THE ETHICAL ENTREPRENEUR

THE ETHICAL ENTREPRENEUR

Succeeding in Business
without Selling Your Soul

PAUL SILBERBERG

New York

THE ETHICAL ENTREPRENEUR
Succeeding in Business without Selling Your Soul

© 2017 **PAUL SILBERBERG**.

Published in New York, New York, by Morgan James Publishing. Morgan James and The Entrepreneurial Publisher are trademarks of Morgan James, LLC.
www.MorganJamesPublishing.com

The Morgan James Speakers Group can bring authors to your live event. For more information or to book an event visit The Morgan James Speakers Group at www.TheMorganJamesSpeakersGroup.com.

Shelfie

A **free** eBook edition is available with the purchase of this print book.

CLEARLY PRINT YOUR NAME ABOVE IN UPPER CASE

Instructions to claim your free eBook edition:
1. Download the Shelfie app for Android or iOS
2. Write your name in **UPPER CASE** above
3. Use the Shelfie app to submit a photo
4. Download your eBook to any device

ISBN 978-1-68350-003-2 paperback
ISBN 978-1-68350-005-6 eBook
ISBN 978-1-68350-004-9 hardcover
Library of Congress Control Number:
2016904322

Author back cover photo by:
Matt Inden

Cover Design by:
Chris Treccani
www.3dogdesign.net

Interior Design by:
Bonnie Bushman
The Whole Caboodle Graphic Design

In an effort to support local communities and raise awareness and funds, Morgan James Publishing donates a percentage of all book sales for the life of each book to Habitat for Humanity Peninsula and Greater Williamsburg.

Get involved today, visit
www.MorganJamesBuilds.com

Habitat
for Humanity®
Peninsula and
Greater Williamsburg
Building Partner

Happy 95th Birthdays, Mom and Dad!

CONTENTS

PREFACE

Some people assert that to build a business you must compromise, or at least defer, certain ethical, family, and communal obligations. They say you'll make up for it later, when you'll have the time and the money.

But my experience and my research tell me that it's in your own self-interest to do it the right way, right from the beginning.

This book is about business: the intersection of entrepreneurship and ethics. It's also a book of stories about lessons I've learned from a few of the spectacular people I've been fortunate to meet along the way.

My business was exclusively devoted to the ultra-high net worth market—entrepreneurs who could afford to invest (and risk) a minimum of $5 million. *Inc.* magazine once called my company "The Ultimate Investment Club for Entrepreneurs." For nearly five decades this "club" included some of the most prominent entrepreneurs in the United States.

Most of these men and women modestly attribute a large part of their success to good luck, being in the right place at the right time. But they recognized opportunity, and they followed their instincts with passion. They took risks. They worked incredibly hard. They capitalized on their innate talents, and they practiced skills that did not come naturally to them. They persisted. They have amazing stories, and their stories are part of my story.

I grew up in middle-class America, in West Caldwell, New Jersey. Both my dad's and my mom's families had been lucky enough, and persistent enough, to escape the pogroms in Poland and Russia and immigrate to the United States in the 1890s. Dad grew up in an American Orthodox Jewish home. Mom's family belonged to the Conservative Jewish Movement, though they were clearly leaning Reform (Granddad's business was importing hams—not at all kosher).

My wife, Aviva, was born in Israel. Her parents were both born in Yemen. In 1943, when Jews were being slaughtered, the rabbis told the Yemenite Jews to get themselves to the city of Aden, where "the wings of an eagle" would take them to the Promised Land. At the time Aviva's folks were teenagers; each walked toward Aden at night with their families and hid during the day—for three months. After they reached Aden, where they met, they lived in a refugee camp for five years. Soon after the State of Israel was established in 1948, they were among the 50,000 Yemenite Jews who were rescued to Israel on Operation Magic Carpet.

Their luck was not just to survive this ordeal, but to be deposited in the remote but scenic village of Ein Kerem outside Jerusalem. There they raised Aviva and her siblings in what I consider a "non-traditional" traditional Orthodox home. There was no running water, no electricity, and no money. There was a gorgeous view and lots of love.

Eight months after I met Aviva in Ein Kerem, we were married near her home. Aviva moved to Philadelphia so that I could continue my career, and all of a sudden the grandson of a ham importer had a kosher home!

This blended background has left its imprint on me and my philosophy of life.

Religion and philosophy aren't usually thought to mix well with business, but what we believe influences the way we behave. Some people think that a person is either ethical, or not. I'll leave it to the philosophers—Aristotle and Aquinas, Darwin and Kant—to focus on the being. I choose to focus on the doing.

Our maker didn't make any of us perfect, but that doesn't mean we shouldn't try to do the right thing. When I look back, I know there are certain things I should have done differently. When I look forward, I know I'll accumulate some more regrets. Hopefully, the process of reflecting on yesterday's stories will help create even better ones tomorrow.

I don't have answers to our ancient philosophical questions, but I do believe this: The ethical entrepreneur has a competitive advantage in attracting the best of the best, and the ethical entrepreneur forges enduring relationships that sustain the business and nourish the soul.

The ethical entrepreneur enjoys a balanced and fulfilling lifestyle, and creates a wealth of values that are transmitted to the community and to the next generation.

The focus of this book is how to position yourself for long-term growth—in your business and in your life.

ACKNOWLEDGMENTS

Aviva is Aviva: No pretenses. Raw emotion. To you, family is everything, and I'm lucky to have said "Yes" when you told me in 1979 that I was going to marry you. Your spicy Yemenite cooking is only a hint of the flavor of living with you. Thank you, Aviva, for always being there for me.

I adore my daughters, Tamar and Tali, as I do my sons-in-law, Yoav and Yoni. I so admire the four of you for who you are and for what you do, including so magnificently parenting your amazing children. I want to thank my nephews, Jonathan and Yoav, who were thoughtful coaches for my first book and my first teaching, as was my daughter Tamar.

How does one thank one's parents? "Thank you" isn't enough for Annice and Sy Silberberg. Their energy and caring continues at the age of ninety-five, thank God! Whatever emphasis one might place on the influence of born versus bred, I'm eternally grateful to Mom and Dad for giving me both my ethical and entrepreneurial foundation, and for setting a standard of commitment and service to community. Sharing both DNA and home were my sisters, Jane Youderian and Amy Brenner, whom I thank for their unwavering support, together with my brother-in-law, John Youderian.

Thirty-six years ago Aviva's parents also became mine. *Todah rabah* (thank you very much), Yedida Yefet, and thank you Ovadia Yefet, one of my quiet but strong role models, though you've been too long a blessed memory. Also too long a blessed memory is my brother-in-law Shaltiel Yefet. Thank you for your love and support: Tehela Nachmani, Bruyah and Adi Shavit, Hemda Yefet, Susan Yefet, and Zvika and Anat Yefet.

In this book I tell stories about some dear friends, each of whom worked tirelessly and patiently with me on my book, in my foray into academia, and in my journey in life. Haim Dahan, Michael Kirschner, Bill Landman, and Robert Schwartz: I'm blessed with your friendship and with your unconditional support. From the bottom of my soul I thank you.

Ed Glickman, Matt Kamens, and Lester Lipschutz: You are more than attorneys and advisors, you are friends and family. You are appreciated and loved. As are Rimon Ben-Shaoul, Angelica Berrie, Steve Fine, Les and Michelle Littman, Jerry Perl, Mimi Schneirov, Elliot Schwartz, Zev Shaposhnick, Stan Sloan, Gil Trachtman, and Yoram "Ya Ya" Yair.

Professionally as well as personally, I can't imagine connecting my dots without Mark Solomon and so many other longtime friends and colleagues, including Meg Abend, John Adams, David "Yemi" Clapper, Cynthia Dill-Pinckney, Senta Fean, Morey Goldberg, Rick Mitchell, Trish Peirce, Mike Sanyour, and Bob Spivak.

How can I thank my new boss, my new mentor, and my old and dear friend, Moshe Porat, Dean of Temple University's Fox School of Business? I'm also indebted to Arvind Parkhe and TL Hill at the Fox School, and to my close friends and members of my ad-hoc academic advisory board, Zvi Grunwald, Allon Guez, and Gabi Szulanski.

Thank you, Jacob "Habibi" Engel; this book would not exist were it not for you, nor would my existence be as meaningful. Ditto to my three rabbis: Yossi Lipsker, "The Rockin' Rabbi" Menachem Schmidt, and Shraga Sherman.

Thanks to these leading entrepreneurs who are not only ethical icons but are always available to help others, including me: Ed Baumstein, Ed Berman, John Bogle, Dave Brennan, David L. Cohen, Don Crawford, Mark Fishman, Mike Frieze, Alan Guttman, Vic Hammel, Andy Heyer, Bob Kogod, Josh Kopelman, John Lehman, Gerry Lenfest, Sandy Lipstein, Skip Loeb, Bernie Marcus, Peter Mullin, Pete Musser, Joe and Jeanette Neubauer, Jim Papada, Jeff Perelman, Larry Plotnick, Ed Satell, Glenn Segal, Ken Sherman, Sandy Solmon, Chuck Steiner, Ron Werner, Josh Weston, and Steve Woodsum.

I'm blessed to find resources who are so talented and relationships so willing to help, so thank you: Alan Boal, Bill Eacho, Terry LaPiere, both Steve Picardes, Neil Raynor, Nancy Reichman, Mal Salter, Michael Shulman, Steve Treat, and Terry White.

I want to acknowledge the memories of some people who enormously impacted my life and who are now "watching" my behavior from a different life: Eli Afriat, Russ Berrie, Allen Bildner, David Blumberg, Eve and Robert Blumberg, Fred Deering, Stan Elkman, David Gerber, Alvin Gutman, Bob Hoagland, Fred Lafer, Phil and Annabelle Lindy, Jim Macaleer, Jerry Mechanick, Zonik Shaham, Ben Silberberg, Bertha Silberberg, and Ed Snider.

I can't imagine an editor more talented or more congenial than Nancy Steele; you amazed me with your wisdom, your work ethic, and your unrelenting commitment to excellence.

Thank you Alex Chadwick, Lawrence Karlson, Jeff Kirschner, and Carole Steinberg. You read the entire manuscript closely and conscientiously, and you offered important comments.

Thank you Mitch Chupak, Oded Hadomi, Adir Kan, Chaim Peri, David Portowicz, and Susan Weijel for your inspiring work in the community, and for inspiring me.

One more essential acknowledgment: *Baruch Hashem* (thank you, God).

Chapter 1

INTEGRITY IS
NON-NEGOTIABLE

W hen I began my career I had little clue where I was headed, but one conversation changed everything.

During my senior year at the University of Pennsylvania I answered an ad in the school paper to interview for a fellowship. The interview turned out to be at the Provident Mutual Life Insurance Company in Philadelphia. The next thing I knew, I was selling life insurance to college kids like myself and to anyone else who would talk with me. My prospects didn't have money, nor were they focused on their mortality. Some fellowship!

I decided to go to law school, but my instincts kept me selling part time. When I was a second-year law student I was introduced to Mark Solomon, who had recently started a company called CMS to sell life insurance to entrepreneurs. Mark said, "Move your insurance practice to CMS and get exposed to a more sophisticated market. When you graduate, if you want to be a lawyer, be a lawyer. If you want to do something in business, who knows, maybe we'll do something together."

That was forty-five years ago. Once CMS became a well-established firm, it was easy to be selective about with whom we did business. But something happened shortly after I started at CMS that became a turning point in my career.

I had been working for months on a large and complicated insurance plan when I learned that Mark refused to do business with that prospect. I was in a panic: We needed that case to pay the rent.

But Mark said, "Don't worry. We'll find people to do business with who share our values. We'll not only figure out how to pay the rent, but at the same time we'll be building a foundation of steel, not of sand. Integrity is non-negotiable."

That was a difficult but important lesson. The good news is that persistence in a personal value system allows you to sleep well at night, and in the long run it pays big dividends.

Relationships in the CMS network are typically twenty, thirty, even forty-plus years, and this values-based, entrepreneurial group of companies produced some extraordinary results. The company morphed into an alternative-investment firm that at its peak employed 120 people. We acquired about $12 billion of assets in addition to an estimated $6 billion of life insurance. It was a blast. Not every day nor every dollar, of course. But my business was certainly one of my passions, I think in large part because it was where my instincts—and my heart—led me.

I followed a similar path in my personal life. On a trip to Israel in 1979, I stepped into a Yemenite home near Jerusalem for a cup of coffee. A week later one of the daughters from that host family told me that we were going to get married. I told her she was crazy. My friends and family back in the States told me I was crazy. But I followed my instincts, and eight months later I was back in Jerusalem, being married to Aviva. That was thirty-six years ago, and it's been a wonderful thirty-six years.

Be a Farmer

Looking back at the times when I met Aviva, when I joined CMS, and when I applied for that fellowship, could I have predicted the outcome? No way. But following my instincts led me in the right direction, and I was lucky enough to have some excellent tutors along the way.

When I was selling life insurance part time, my supervisor at Provident Mutual was a retired Marine drill sergeant. He wouldn't let me finish my week until I had booked my quota of appointments for the coming week. Can you imagine, at ten p.m. on a Friday night, how I felt when my friends were partying and I was dialing for dollars, cold-calling for life insurance appointments?

That's when I learned to spell "No" with a "g"—Go. *No means go*. My drill sergeant taught me that every "No" brought me closer to a "Yes."

Persistence is important not only to one's work ethic. More importantly, persistence is essential in maintaining one's moral ethic. The CMS perspective was that the world is made up of two types of people: miners and farmers. Miners take out. Farmers take out, but also put back. CMS's investors, joint-venture partners, and employees were farmers who gave back to society, or they were not accepted as part of the CMS family. The responsibility of our own company and our employees to give back is the heart of the CMS Credo (Appendix 1).

Making a contribution to the community is a responsibility that can't be delegated, and it shouldn't be deferred. I lost my brother-in-law at age thirty-four, and one of my best friends at fifty-two, so I know that life is too short to procrastinate.

Don't defer your farming responsibilities. Whatever financial pressures you feel now should be tempered by knowing there are so many less fortunate. Make your charitable contributions off the top line; don't wait to see if there's money left over on the bottom line. And don't wait to volunteer until you feel that the time is convenient.

I'm fortunate to have known some of our country's most spectacularly successful businessmen and businesswomen, and in this book you'll find samples of their wisdom. The true measure of their success, however, is in how they carried out their leadership and entrepreneurship—with their refusal to compromise their ethics, and with their demonstration that good ethics are good business.

Chapter 2

YOUR CLIENT COMES FIRST

I n the right context, an old idea can be revolutionary.
In 1969, when I was an undergraduate at the University of
Pennsylvania and working part time selling life insurance, I
had a supervisor, Joe Patton, who was indeed Patton-esque. After
twenty years' service in the Marine Corps he was well qualified for
his job of kicking the you-know-what out of newly recruited life
insurance agents.

One day Joe suggested that I "consider" attending a lecture
sponsored by the Philadelphia Association of Life Underwriters.
Joe told me, "The speaker is one of the country's most famous life
insurance salesmen, a young guy who happens to be based right
here in Philadelphia."

I showed up at the designated hotel directly from class, wearing my undergrad uniform of jeans and T-shirt. At twenty-two, I was by a quarter-century the youngest of 500 insurance agents in the room. All of them were men; all of them were wearing gray suits with red-and-blue rep-striped ties over white button-down shirts; all of them had short, greying crew cuts.

That was the Vietnam era. I thought I was standing at the end of some factory assembly line conveyor belt that was endlessly dropping off cardboard cutouts of life-sized insurance agents. And all of them were holding black briefcases, all exactly the same size and shape.

The featured speaker was Mark Solomon, a thirty-one-year-old hippie with long hair that curled over his shoulders. He wore a wild, bright blue, yellow-checkered suit with a crazy red-and-orange flowered tie. I thought there must have been a mistake: Either the hotel had the wrong speaker on this particular stage, or the wrong audience for this particular speaker. But once Mark started talking, everyone in the room was mesmerized, including me.

Mark Solomon's message was that an insurance agent should have only one boss, and that boss should be the client, not the insurance company. This was radical. At that time nearly all life insurance policies were sold by sales agencies owned by life insurance companies. I'd bet that almost every one of the salesmen in the room that day was an agent for a big insurer such as Provident Mutual, Prudential, or Metropolitan.

The Best Product

The illusion permitted by the industry was this: The agent was allowed to present himself as an independent broker who claimed to be searching the market for the best product. In fact, the insurance companies did allow you to sell other companies' products, as long as you didn't sell too many of them! An agent signed what we in the field called a "slave contract" with an insurance company. After some initial training subsidy, you were rewarded with large upfront commissions, followed by a like amount of renewal commissions typically paid over the next ten years. But the renewal commissions were not vested.

Then—and now—most salespeople live off commissions. This means that the less you sell, the more you starve. It's one thing when you're a twenty-two-year-old undergrad with no dependents, and lucky enough (as was I) to be supported by your folks. What about the other 499 salespeople listening that day to Mark Solomon? As I said, they were middle-aged guys, and they had to feed their families. The more they sold, the larger their renewal commission account. The larger their renewal account, the more captive they became.

What would you do if you were selling life insurance and your primary company's products became uncompetitive? If you followed your heart—and your fiduciary responsibility to serve your client's interests—you'd sell another company's products. The problem is that if you got caught, you'd be fired. You'd lose your renewal commissions along with your job. If you had a wife, kids, and a mortgage, you'd be in trouble. This is not theory; this actually happened. Unfortunately, it still does, though not as often.

In our industry Mark Solomon's position was revolutionary. I'm surprised that the trade association, which was controlled by the big insurance companies, allowed him to speak. They knew what he was going to say, and he said it: "Your client always comes first. You cannot have dual loyalty to both an insurance company and to your client."

Mark's prescription: "You should sign an independent brokerage contract instead of a sales agency contract. Yes, you will receive lower commissions, but you will own the renewals. Only then will you own your independence. Only then can you truly shop the market and make appropriate recommendations to your client."

Today it's called "alignment of interests." Since biblical times it's been called doing the right thing.

I wonder how many people sitting in that room changed their behavior as a result of Mark's speech. I can only speak for one. I thought about a lot of things at that time: girls; how to get through school; girls; how to sell the next insurance policy; girls. I also thought a lot about my part-time life insurance business.

I had three aspirations at the time. First, I wanted to sell insurance to anybody who would talk to me so I could make some money. Second, I wanted to figure out how to sell insurance to successful entrepreneurs.

Third, I didn't want to be a slave. Every year at the Passover Seder we Jews remind ourselves that we were freed from slavery in Egypt thousands of years ago. Mark's analogy impacted me.

Yes, I wanted to make money, but not at the expense of my independence, and not at the cost of not doing the right thing for my clients.

The next year I started law school, which accelerated my self-perception as a professional. My part-time cold calling to sell life insurance became blended with a calling to represent clients. I was introduced to Mark two years after I heard him speak. After our initial meeting at a restaurant, Mark invited me to visit CMS. That was November, 1971. Mark had started the firm two years earlier, in a beautiful old converted townhouse near Philadelphia's Rittenhouse Square. I allocated an hour for my visit. I left eight hours later. A month later—December, 1971—I got a desk behind a file cabinet and signed a brokerage contract with CMS Companies, with vested renewal commissions.

Chapter 3

CHOOSE SUCCESS

D o you believe in fate? How do you connect the dots when you think about what you hope will happen in your life . . . and what the future will bring?

As I was preparing a commencement address I'd been invited to give to graduates of Temple University's Fox School of Business, I turned to YouTube to revisit the speech that Steve Jobs delivered at Stanford University in 2005.[1] My friend Moshe Porat, the widely acclaimed Dean of the Fox School, subsequently suggested that I watch another commencement address, this one by Lewis Katz. "Really? Enough already," I thought. As it turned out, Lewis Katz's speech at Temple University in June 2014 is extremely thought-provoking as well as entertaining.[2]

Lewis Katz didn't become as famous as Steve Jobs. He grew up poor in Camden, New Jersey, but he became a billionaire, thanks in part to his ownership of parking garages, billboards, and "yes," the New York Yankees, and the YES television network. I met him only casually over the years, but knew that he was always generous with his time and his money. His message: "self-confidence . . . patience . . . grit . . . but don't sell your soul to the workplace."

Two weeks after he gave that speech, Katz died in a plane crash. He was seventy-two. Did Steve Jobs have an advantage in that he knew—at age fifty—that he was dying of cancer? Or was Lewis Katz the lucky one because he did not know he was about to die?

Knowing that few of us can predict when we will die, how can we use this knowledge—or more accurately, lack of knowledge!—to optimize whatever allocation of time we do have? Here are a few other fundamental questions:

- If you want to be an entrepreneur, do you have what it takes?
- Is it enough to be willing to work hard and persist?
- Must you have inherited certain genetic traits in order to be successful?
- Can you learn enough entrepreneurial skills to tilt the scale in favor of your success?
- Can you connect enough of the dots looking forward to feel that you are headed in the right direction?

Every successful entrepreneur has unique stories about knockdowns. Here's one of Katz's:

I learned at the very young age of twenty, if you don't believe in yourself, nobody else will. . . . That's not to say that there won't be knockdowns. Life has taught me that the only way to win when you're knocked down is to get up, dust yourself off, and go back into the race.

When I was a kid, I dreamed of being an NBA player, but after being cut from my junior high school team and my high school team, I realized the only way I wasn't going to get cut was if I bought an NBA team. We bought the New Jersey Nets, my partners and I, in 1998. One week after buying it, the players went on strike. The NBA shut down, and they canceled half of the season—we quickly lost millions of dollars.

Knockdown Number One.

. . . . The governor said, "If you want to build a new arena in Newark, New Jersey, you have to have two teams." So, we bought the New Jersey Devils, and we lost more millions.

Knockdown Number Two.

Finally, somebody suggested that if we could merge the baseball team, which played six months from April to October, with the basketball team, which played November through May, we could start a television network by showing those two teams. So our partnership bought half of . . . the New York Yankees and . . . we started something called YES. It became the most successful regional sports network in history, and we sold it to Fox Sports, and then we didn't lose.[3]

Katz often said, "The message is patience, and the message is grit." My interpretation of patience in this context is persistence—with a sense of urgency, tempered by a long-term perspective.

I don't know any successful entrepreneur who doesn't have grit. Many entrepreneurs fail simply because they're not willing to pay the price, to do what they have to do to succeed.

Malcolm S. Salter of the Harvard Business School has said that "strategy is 20 percent conception and 80 percent execution."[4]

The most successful entrepreneurs I know work harder than anyone else. This means being willing to get on a plane and sit beside a client just to be able to have a twenty-minute conversation, even if it means investing in a round-trip flight that takes most of a day. It also means making the right ethical decision even when it's a hard choice.

Your Own Free Will
How much of a role do you think luck and timing will play in your life, compared with your ability to impact events, your "free choice?" One of my entrepreneurial heroes, Philadelphia's Glenn Segal, told me, "God puts you in the right place, but doesn't do the deal for you."[5]

Glenn is a big believer in free will, though he's not an absolutist. I asked him, "What's your number, using a scale of one to ten? Number ten represents the relative importance of free will, where the number one represents 100 percent genetic influence." Glenn's number was seven. This bias toward the importance of free choice is found among many of the classic commentators on entrepreneurship. For example, Michael E. Gerber, in *The E-Myth Revisited,* wrote, "great businesses are not built by extraordinary people, but by ordinary people doing extraordinary things."[6]

The dean of business writers, Peter F. Drucker, took an even stronger position on the importance of free choice in his book, *The Effective Executive.* "I have not come across a single 'natural,' an executive who was born effective," Drucker wrote. "All the effective ones have had to learn to be effective."[7] (Would it be cynical to point out that Drucker was in the business of teaching executives to be effective?)

Opposing experts can be found in the genetics camp, such as Arnold Daniels, creator of the behavioral science-based Predictive Index. The PI, as it's often called, has been widely applied in the workplace since 1955, and I used it in my business for twenty years. Daniels said that if you're not born with a certain drive and an acute sense of urgency, you should look for a job rather than try to create jobs. He did concede the potential to temper some personality-based behaviors, but he maintained that "some kinds of change must be considered impossible."[8]

Maybe Daniels would give me a score of two on my one-to-ten scale of genetics versus free will. I'm probably a four—a reflection of my genetic legacy. My father, Sy, had a dental practice in our home town of West Caldwell, New Jersey, and when he sold his practice to his partners at the age of sixty-five, he started a new business that ultimately provided dental services to more than thirty nursing homes in northern New Jersey. Whether by inheritance or osmosis, his business sense seems to have found its way to me.

I began my first business venture when I was in kindergarten. My father's dental practice was on the first floor of a building just around the corner from Caldwell's main street, Bloomfield Avenue, the busiest street in that quiet little town. One day the proprietor of one of the shops along Bloomfield Avenue saw me walking down the street all alone. Taking me by the hand, he led me back to the safety of my father's office. In answer to my father's questions, I had to confess: I'd taken a handful of his business cards from his office and was selling them—at a nickel each. I was disappointed that my enterprise had come to an end, because by then I'd earned almost a quarter!

Born or bred, most entrepreneurs have a lot of fun along the way. You can see it in the commencement videos of both Lewis Katz and Steve Jobs.

The entrepreneurs I consider most successful also make a commitment to give back.

In his commencement address Katz said,

Make every effort in your life to make a difference. Remember: Success is not about material things. Watch,

study people you admire. . . . Work matters, but family
matters more. Don't sell your soul to the workplace. . . .
Make time for those who need you, and for the causes you
believe in. . . . Don't give away your time to fools, because
you never get it back.[9]

One of my pet peeves is hearing people say, "I don't have
enough time." That's simply not true. You have all there is.

Since we know that our time is finite, the only pertinent
question is how we choose to allocate it each day. If you're a "free
will" person, will it on! If you believe that fate will determine your
opportunities, be alert to them and seize them as best you can.
When your final day comes, you want to be able to look back with
satisfaction on how you connected the dots.

Chapter 4

IT'S NEVER TOO LATE
TO INNOVATE

Bernie Marcus was forty-eight when he was fired from a company called Handy Dan. John Bogle was forty-four when he was fired from Wellington Management Company.

At age forty-nine, Bernie Marcus created a new industry—big-box retailing. His company: The Home Depot.

At age forty-five, John Bogle created a new industry—low-cost, passive index funds. His company: The Vanguard Group.

In the business world, metrics do "count," though I believe they speak a bit too loudly. Bernie and his two partners started The Home Depot in 1978; its revenues exceeded $80 billion in 2015. Home Depot is the largest home-improvement retailer in the world. It beat its biggest competitor, Lowe's, by 60 percent.

John Bogle started Vanguard in 1974. In 2015 it managed more than $3 trillion. Vanguard is the largest mutual fund company in the world. It beat its biggest competitor, Fidelity, by about 80 percent.[1]

Both Bernie Marcus and John Bogle are entrepreneurial icons, for sure. More important, they are ethical icons. They both believe that their ethics were an essential ingredient for their entrepreneurial success. I believe that too.

Though they represent vastly different personalities, backgrounds, and industries, these two entrepreneurs share traits that are instructive for all of us.

I've been fortunate to know Bernie Marcus pretty well, for a pretty long period of time. He's CMS's most famous investor, for nearly thirty years. I've known John Bogle only casually, through the Philadelphia community. I've watched him on TV, heard many of his speeches, and read most of his ten books, including one of my favorite books of all time, *Enough: True Measures of Money, Business, and Life.*

I've also enjoyed a long professional and personal relationship with John Bogle's son-in-law, Scott Renninger. Not all relationships ripen with age. Fortunately, Scott's and mine has. Scott is quite a successful investor in his own right; his company is called Independence Asset Advisors. I know, from Scott, how wisely John Bogle invested in his family.[2] As prolific as John was professionally—building Vanguard, writing books, giving TV interviews, lecturing at universities, working relentlessly in the community—in my eyes, John's real fame was just being there for his family.

I know, from employees at Vanguard, that John is always accessible to them. I also know, from son-in-law Scott, that John is always there for his family, including six kids and a dozen grandchildren. John's investment in his family yielded an inheritance of values that have been handed down in his family from generation to generation. To do this right requires a lot of time and energy. But I'll bet this is John's only investment about which he would *not* say, "enough."

For the aspiring entrepreneur, it's never too late to innovate. Look what John Bogle did at age forty-five, and what Bernie Marcus did at age forty-nine. If you're a little anxious about your next step, hang in there. Persevere. Spell "No" with a "g." When you get knocked down, get back up.

Very few of us can become as successful as Bernie Marcus or John Bogle, but we can achieve more than we dream of—if only we try.

Chapter 5

AS GOOD AS YOUR WORD

When you say you're going to do something, do it!
Words are very important. But actions are more
so. The rules are simple:

- If you're not going to do something, don't say you will.
- If you do say you're going to do something, you must do it.
- If it turns out that you can't do it, or if you change your mind and you don't want to do it, or if something comes up and you need to defer doing it, you must communicate with those impacted, as quickly as possible.

Once you commit to do something—anything!—silence is no longer an option.

Two more things:

- Under no circumstances should you say one thing but do the opposite. Hypocrisy and leadership do not mix.
- This doesn't mean you can't make a mistake, or that you can't change your mind. Just be open and forthright. And be sure to get back to those on the other end immediately.

A Promise Kept

If you're a hockey fan, you're familiar with the legendary Bobby Clarke, who led the Philadelphia Flyers to win the Stanley Cup in 1974 and 1975. Bobby then became the general manager of the team, which was owned by businessman, philanthropist, and sports fanatic Ed Snider.

I'm not much of a sports fan, except during the fair—and unfortunately, rare—weather when a Philadelphia team is in contention. But even I heard the rumors in the late 1990s that Bobby Clarke was leaving the City of Brotherly Love. I was shocked when I got a phone call that Ed Snider wanted to meet with me.

Ed recalled a conversation that had occurred more than twenty years earlier, during the height of the Flyers Stanley Cup success, when Bobby Clarke was negotiating his contract. Ed told me that during the negotiations he had said, "Don't worry, Bobby. I'll take care of you for the rest of your life."

"Did you say that?" I asked Ed.

"Yes."

"Is there anything written?"

"No."

"What does that mean: 'Don't worry, I'll take care of you for the rest of your life?'" I asked.

"That's what I want you to tell us," said Ed. "I want you to figure out a fair deal. I want Bobby Clarke to feel it's a fair deal. I said it. I gave my word. I want to keep my word. I just have no idea what those words mean!"[1]

Neither did I, and I argued that we were not the people to help him solve this riddle. Ed said, "You were referred to me by someone I trust. You're reputed to be smart and honest. One of your businesses revolves around executive compensation. I have an executive who needs to be compensated. I'm not going anywhere else."

I responded, "Ed, you've been on our target prospect list for some time. We cannot charge you a fee for a project outside our expertise. But we will work on this project as a way for you to sample our thinking. If we can help you solve this problem, and if you like our thinking, our fee will be the opportunity to try to get you to buy some insurance through us or to invest with us."

I remember coming back to the office, frantically searching for our analyst, Morey Goldberg. Over the July 4 weekend Morey and I worked intensively. We interviewed Bobby Clarke and worked closely with Ed Snider's longtime confidante and extremely talented CFO, Sandy Lipstein. Then we came up with a plan that both Bobby and Ed accepted.

Ed Snider proved himself to be not only an extremely successful entrepreneur but a highly ethical leader.

If you were Ed Snider, what would you have done?

Little Things Count Big

The most successful entrepreneurs I've known are meticulous about keeping their word.

Forbes estimates Bernie Marcus's net worth in the range of $3.5 to $5.5 billion. Though he looks like a sixty-six-year-old—and acts like one—he's actually *eighty*-six. Although he retired as The Home Depot's Chairman of the Board in 2002, he's as busy as anyone I know, and he really didn't need to schlep from his home in Florida to Philadelphia in the middle of winter to speak to students at Temple University, where I was teaching a class at the Fox School of Business. Nevertheless, he agreed to do so, and all the plans were made for February 10, 2016.

Just before New Year's, Bernie sent me an email via his executive assistant, Leslie King.

The following excerpts from our quick exchange offer some lessons to be learned from Bernie:[2]

On December 28, 2015, Leslie wrote:

Bernie asked that I reach out to you ASAP in regards to the seminar in February. Bernie now has to be in Israel the afternoon of Thursday, February 11th for an important meeting with the Israel Democracy Institute. In order for him to arrive by 4:00 PM Israeli time, he needs to depart out of Atlanta on Wednesday, February 10th by 6:00 PM ET.

I know you have made all the plans and the agenda for the seminar, but we need to somehow work this so Bernie is able to leave Philadelphia in time to arrive in Atlanta, allow the plane to refuel, and depart for Israel at 6:00 PM.

Please let me know your thoughts and how we can work this?

Later that day I replied:

Want to try for Tuesday Feb 9? Or Wednesday Feb 3?

The next day Leslie wrote:

Bernie said the 9th will work out just fine. He wasn't sure if the private dialogue that was scheduled for 6:00 PM included dinner? If not, he suggested the two of you have dinner together? He will plan on flying to Israel on the 10th.

On New Year's Eve I responded:

We're on for Tue Feb 9: 4:00 PM speech to a couple hundred students/guests at Temple University Main Campus; 5:30 PM class with my 25 students; then 7:00 PM small dinner with Bernie, me and Dean Moshe Porat, plus three of my MBA students picked by lottery.

Or Bernie could just rest. Not such a terrible idea, particularly since he has to be back in Atlanta by 6:00 PM Feb 10, so he can then fly to Israel to do some other good stuff for the world. Come on, Leslie, he *is* eighty-four! (I concede, he doesn't look it, and he doesn't act it, but check his birth certificate.)

Within hours, Leslie King confirmed:

We will figure all this out next week or so. But, just to clear things up—Bernie is actually eighty-six! You would never believe it though, as he has more stamina and energy than anyone I know!

———————————

Here are the takeaways:

- Whatever you do in life, do it with class—personally, professionally, philanthropically—publicly and privately.
- Note Bernie's humility. Many so-called leaders hide behind, and take pains to reference, big names. Bernie never named the dignitaries he needed to meet in Israel: Prime Minister Benjamin Netanyahu and former U.S. Secretary of State George Shultz, among others. Actions do speak louder than words.
- Most important, take your commitments seriously.

As I said earlier—and as I'll say again, a hundred times—if you tell someone you're going to do something, just do it!

My Israeli Brother
The people I admire most are those who keep their promises and fulfill their goals. One of the beautiful benefits of philanthropy is that you meet some amazing people. If you're lucky, and if you work at it, some of them can become your best friends. That's what happened with Haim and me.

Haim Dahan is someone who does what he says he'll do. I met him in 1999, when he and I helped Bernie Marcus recruit for a fundraising mission to Israel to support the Israel Democracy Institute (IDI). Haim and I bonded on that bus in Israel. Since then I call him Achie, which is Hebrew for "my brother." To use that nickname is a high compliment; you can't choose your sibling, but you can choose your friend.

Haim was born in Casablanca, Morocco, in 1960. His family immigrated to Israel when he was two. When he was twenty-seven, he moved to Atlanta to pursue his PhD in computers and engineering. He needed to make some money, so he got a job at IBM. At age thirty-one he started his own supply-chain software company, which in itself could be a whole book about entrepreneurial success.

Haim used to tell me that he wanted to raise his children in Israel. "When I sell my business, I'm going to take my money and my kids and move back to Israel," he'd say. I'd heard that mantra a thousand times from many Israelis who were living in the U.S. Many of them really believe they will return to Israel. Many want to; many intend to; very few do.

I totally get it: Life in America is good. So is life in Israel, but it's harder. It's harder to do business in Israel than in America. And in America, your kids don't have to serve in the Army, at least not at the moment.

Though I usually believe whatever Haim tells me, in this case I did not. But as 1999 drew to a close Haim sold his company, and in 2000 he brought his kids "home" to Israel. This was unusual under any circumstances, but what made it extraordinary was that the Second Intifada had started. There was a major uprising by the Palestinians. Violence was the norm during those dark days. Unfortunately, one can make the case that what was then, was also before, is today, and will be tomorrow—the new normal? But one thing is for sure: At that time, it was *not* normal for anyone to travel to Israel, let alone for a family to return there.

Haim did exactly what he said he was going to do, and under the most trying of circumstances. I thought to myself, "Here's a man of his word."

Despite the distance—or maybe because of it, which required us to make more of an effort—our friendship grew. Part of it was our common commitment to at-risk children in Israel. We volunteered together for many years on behalf of a residential youth village named Yemin Orde. We collaborated for a dozen years on Ofanim, a non-governmental organization founded by Haim to use old buses—and new technology, and passionate instructors— to provide mobile labs and encouragement to children in Israel's periphery. (I call it "the bus deal.")

Part of the glue for the bond between Haim and me is that I periodically visit Israel, and he periodically visits the States. We find a place to sneak a cigar (don't tell my cardiologist!) and a nice Malbec. As a "condition precedent" to Haim marrying Shirley, both she and my wife Aviva agreed that once a year "their boys" would be able to run away together for a week. Haim and I visited Buenos Aires, the source of Malbec. We skied all over the world, wherever and whenever we could find snow. We visited Bucharest in Romania, and Sofia in Bulgaria; Irkutsk in Siberia, and Ulan

Bator in Mongolia; Petra in Jordan, and Paris in France, sometimes with family and friends, but often just the two of us.

Haim's business success is well documented, and he's an ethical doer who in 2015 was recognized as Israel's "most effective social entrepreneur" by a joint project of Israeli nonprofit organizations.

The Value of Trust

Haim is also an ethical entrepreneur, as I know from experience. In 2015 I committed to invest in one of his new ventures. Haim had maxed out on how much of his own capital he was willing to put into this start-up, and he needed additional investors. My wire transfer was literally to be sent in an hour when he called.

"Paul, I just learned of a potential issue regarding one of the minority partners," he told me. "I don't think it will impact the company. I'm continuing with it." But then he said, "I know you weren't enthused with this deal to begin with. This change morally releases you from any prior commitment. You can reconsider, if you want."

I did reconsider, and I chose not to invest. I hope Haim hits a home run on this one. He deserves to, and it may happen. Generally speaking, I'm really not comfortable with venture capital—I don't understand technology; I don't like early-stage investing; I don't like the paperwork; I don't want to take the risk—so I was happy not to participate. But I was happiest about, though not surprised by, Haim's ethical response.

Haim can raise any amount of money he wants, and can gain access to any businessperson he'd like to meet, because people trust him. He earns that trust every day, which allows him to earn more for himself, for his family, and for his philanthropy. If and when he wants to.

After a newspaper article announced that one of Haim's and my friends had sold one of his companies for a lot of money, Haim had the following exchange with him over dinner. This friend is hyper-competitive. Haim teased him:

"I'm wealthier than you," said Haim.

"Why do you say that?" asked the friend, somewhat skeptically, and somewhat jealously.

"Because I have something that you don't," said Haim.

"What's that?" asked the friend, more inquisitive, and more engaged.

"I have enough," said Haim. [3]

I had recently given Haim the book *Enough* by John Bogle, founder of Vanguard. John asks us to consider the meaning of the word in our businesses, our money, and our lives. Haim is clearly in the John Bogle camp: Enough is enough!

I did invest in one start-up with Haim. I like to talk with him when I'm exercising on my elliptical. With the seven-hour time difference between Philadelphia and Tel Aviv, I can usually find a time convenient for him, and it makes my time on the elliptical go faster. Haim was updating me about one of his start-ups, and told me that he was grappling with an ethical and business issue with one of his investors.

"I'll buy that guy out," I told Haim.

"Really?" asked Haim.

"Yes," I said.

Haim said, "You'll come in at the investor's original valuation from five years ago."

A few weeks later Haim said, "It looks like the issue is resolved. I'm going to sell the company. Congratulations, you made three times your money."

"What are you talking about?" I said. "I haven't made any investment yet. I haven't sent you any money. I haven't seen any documents. An investment starts when an investor goes at risk."

"I know that, but you agreed to invest, so you're an investor," said Haim.

This led to one of our few heated arguments. Haim insisted that he was going to send me the profits—not an unsubstantial sum—whereas I insisted that I had not yet invested, so I was not entitled to any profits.

What would you have done in these circumstances if you were Haim?

What if you'd been me?

As it turned out, Haim decided not to sell the company. He resolved the issue with the other shareholder, who opted to keep his money in the company. Haim also took my money to help grow the company. I became the new shareholder, but at the old valuation.

The final chapter of this story has not yet been written. However, when Haim founded this company, he made sure that one of the original shareholders was Ofanim, the nonprofit that provides education to the children of Israel's periphery.

Like Bernie Marcus and John Bogle, Haim Dahan is a man of his word. Each one gives a lot. And each of them will tell you—as they tell me—that they receive much more than they give.

Chapter 6

DON'T MANAGE—LEAD!

G reat leaders attract top talent, but the secret to great leadership has nothing to do with authority.

In 2015 I was part of a group to have the honor of meeting Shimon Peres, the Nobel prize-winner who had served not only as prime minister of Israel, the position that wields the power in that democracy, but also as Israel's president, an important but ceremonial position. Twelve of us—six Americans, six Israelis—were visiting Tel Aviv on behalf of at-risk children in Israel, and we met for an hour with Shimon Peres in his office.

Entrepreneurship was not on the agenda, but leadership certainly was. He told us:

> When I was prime minister I had all the authority in the world, and I accomplished nothing.
>
> When I was president I had no authority, and I accomplished a great deal.[1]

What does this have to do with entrepreneurship?

To be a successful entrepreneur, it helps if you can manage people. If you have authority, you can supervise people. However, if you want to manage them well, it will help if you understand who they are—and who you are.

Recognize and Respect Differences

Twenty years ago I called on a successful businesswoman in Boston who was a potential investor in CMS. I was startled when the first thing she said to me was, "Would you mind filling out a short personality survey? It'll take less than ten minutes. There's no right or wrong. We routinely use it with all our vendors, employees, and other professionals."

It sounded pretty weird, but I said, "Why not?"

When I returned a few weeks later for our second meeting, she gave me the results of the survey, which is called The Predictive Index. She then proceeded to describe me as if she'd known me all my life. I said, "You must have spoken with one of my business partners, or my wife, or my mother?" She said, "If you'd like to learn more about this survey, call my PI guy."

The next day I called Steve Picarde at The Predictive Index. After our conversation I was still skeptical, but I gave the survey to ten people at my company, from principal to messenger. I then sent these surveys to Steve. In those days the surveys and the analyses were done manually, but now, of course, it's all computerized and instantaneous.

Steve had never met me nor any of our employees, but when he gave me the results over the phone, he described these ten people to a T. It was as if he had worked side by side with me for years. (My PI says I'm an introvert, but I'm so assertive and so goal-oriented that I often act as an extrovert. I also have an acute sense of urgency and compulsive attention to detail. For PI aficionados, I'm a "high A, low B, low C, high D.")

Since then, my company never hired any employee without first getting his or her PI. We showed the results to each person and watched him or her share our amazement at how accurately—though not perfectly—a ten-minute word-association survey could paint a portrait of a personality.

A Powerful Tool

Steve always preached to me that the PI was not a predictor of success, but should be viewed as only one tool to collect pre-employment data, together with information about education, work experience, specialized training, and intelligence.

Our experience at CMS confirmed that we could not rely on PI as a predictor of success, but during the past twenty years we did find it to be 100 percent accurate in predicting failure. Failure did not mean that an individual was not a good entrepreneur or executive or employee. It simply meant that he or she was not a good fit for the position we needed to fill.

Whenever we hired a candidate despite a red light in the PI, it invariably did not work out. When we looked back, we always saw how the PI had correctly warned us that this person would not be a good fit for a certain position. After far too many mistakes, we learned to rely on the PI when the red light was flashing.

Our management team at CMS used to take two-day PI retreats to learn how to interact with one another more effectively. In 2014 I had a conversation with CMS's Chief Financial Officer, David Clapper. David told me that one of the reasons he and I worked so well together, particularly during the highly stressful financial crisis of 2008 and 2009, was because Steve Picarde had explained my PI to our group. David said, "He specifically advised me that I should try to avoid detailed, technical discussions, and just give you the bottom line. On the other hand, Steve told you to be sensitive to my PI, that there will be times I will need you to hear me out on the whys and wherefores. We both worked on that, and it worked well."[2]

To this day, my associates at CMS and I continue to reference PI, as do members of my immediate family—my wife, our two daughters, and our two sons-in-law. (I wonder at what age we should introduce our grandchildren to PI?) Although I know I seem like a promoter, I have zero financial interest in Predictive Index. I am just a PI zealot. This amazing tool can be used not only to hire better, but also to better understand, and to better manage, your key people. Including yourself.

Leadership must be earned. Shimon Peres earned the power to lead not through his formal authority but through the combined aptitudes, attitudes, empathy, and ethics that characterized his distinctive personality.

To earn the power to lead, you must learn to know your own personality, and you must learn how to understand others. The PI can help you do both.

The PI is not a predictor of ethical behavior. Steve Picarde believes that some correlations can be observed in this regard, but they're subtle. Nevertheless, I enthusiastically recommend this tool to help you build your leadership skills and your business. There's good reason that the PI has been translated into 68 languages and is used in 142 countries.

Invest in Your Support Staff

One measure of your leadership ability is the quality of your support staff. Excellent leaders attract and retain excellent employees because they understand and appreciate the importance of their whole team. Egomaniacs feel their success is solely attributable to themselves; ethical entrepreneurs know the truth.

If you have an assistant, you can test yourself by making a rigorous examination of your role in that relationship. If you've had a series of assistants, but they keep leaving, look closely in the mirror. If your assistant has been with you for a long period of time, but isn't really happy, maybe she or he just can't afford to leave. Either way, it might be time to invest some of your time and money in meeting with an executive coach or psychologist.

Investing in an executive coach can make all the difference to a subpar performer, which in turn can make all the difference to a company. I watched the following story unfold: It had a happy ending, though it looked like a disaster in the making. An assistant to one of my friend's most productive executives was being treated poorly by her boss. The executive was courteous to anyone he considered his equal or superior, but was downright rude—almost abusive—to other employees, including his own assistant.

The CEO had numerous heart-to-heart conversations with the executive. He promised to change his behavior, and he did. For a while. Then he reverted to his old pattern. They talked again. And again: He promised; he changed his behavior; he reverted.

The company needed this guy's production, but his misbehavior was unacceptable. Finally the CEO said: See an executive coach and learn to behave appropriately, or leave the firm.

It was a tough conversation, but the executive agreed to see a coach. It required a significant investment of time, money, and energy, but the return on investment was excellent, both for the executive and for the company.

Investing in your support staff also means providing positive feedback. Some of the smartest people in the world don't realize how important this is: All of us, even the most assured, have frail human egos that need reassurance. An expression of recognition for a job well done, or even an outstanding effort, costs nothing and reaps rewards of mutual respect and appreciation.

Doing the right thing for your support staff is not only the right thing to do, but it pays. If you don't yet have a staff to support your efforts, work hard—and work honestly—and soon enough, you will.

Chapter 7

TEN TRAITS TO TAKE
YOU TO THE TOP

O ne of my hometown superheroes is Philadelphian David L. Cohen. David is a spectacular leader, a highly ethical entrepreneur, and an amazing human being.

On the professional side, he's Senior Executive Vice President of Comcast Corporation/NBCUniversal. In his "spare" time David chairs the University of Pennsylvania's Board of Trustees and actively volunteers in a host of other educational, civic, and charitable activities. Nobody who knows David knows how he manages to do it all, and to do it all so well.

David is one of the few people in the United States who successfully ran a major city; he was chief of staff to Philadelphia mayor Edward G. Rendell from 1992 to 1997. No amount of earnings could compensate David for the time, energy, and leadership that he commits to causes he believes in, particularly when it comes to educating and mentoring young people. Giving back is not a new phenomenon to David; I saw him do exactly the same thing when he was a "start-up" struggling young lawyer.

You can find hundreds of "top ten" lists for entrepreneurs, but I'll save you the trouble by sharing David Cohen's list of the top ten most valuable traits for successful entrepreneurs:[1]

1. Humility
2. A sense of humor
3. An ability to inspire
4. Vision
5. An ability to communicate
6. Flexibility
7. A habit of leading by example
8. A willingness to show appreciation
9. Team-building skills
10. The ability to maintain perspective

David is one of the top executives of the world's largest broadcasting and cable company. Notice which quality he lists first. When I asked him why he puts humility at the top of the list, he said, "Great leaders never ask of others what they won't do themselves."

Like many other qualities, humility can be an acquired trait. If you have any doubt, ask Pope Francis; if you cannot ask the Pope, read *Lead with Humility: 12 Leadership Lessons from Pope Francis* by Jeffrey A. Krames. Its author claims the Pope "misses no opportunity to show . . . that people *can learn* to be more humble."[2]

A word of caution: Humility is a good thing, but false humility is a lie. That may seem like a very thin line, but it's transparent to most people.

Keep Your Perspective

Without the ability to maintain perspective, even the most gifted entrepreneur will miss a wealth of opportunities.

Peter Mullin is probably the world's leading expert on executive benefits, as well as one of the smartest, nicest, most effective, most entrepreneurial leaders I've ever met.

Peter also has been an extraordinary friend, client, partner, and advisor. One of my big shortcomings at CMS was not following some of Peter's advice. But I wrote down—and often think about—Peter Mullin's words from a meeting more than thirty years ago:

The urgent always gets in the way of the important.

When you look back, it will not be the first million dollars you earned, nor the first million dollars of assets you accumulated.

What will matter are two things: the relationships made and kept, with the emphasis on kept; and the unforgettable experiences, shared with these people, you can't forget.[3]

Chapter 8
SHARE THE RISK

B eing an entrepreneur means taking risks—but if you decide to share the risks, how will you share the rewards? At CMS Companies, our niche was always building deep relationships with successful entrepreneurs. I define entrepreneur broadly, as someone who is, or was, helping to lead his or her own business, grow a family business, or lead some part of someone else's business, private or public. In other words, I think of an entrepreneur as someone who is or was acting entrepreneurially!

CMS's initial business was selling life insurance to successful entrepreneurs. Although our clients were wealthy by almost any metric, in the 1970s their fiscal wealth consisted mostly of bricks and mortar, or stock in a company with limited liquidity. At that time, the one asset our clients didn't have was cash.

Once they covered their living expenses, every last nickel they could earn or borrow was reinvested to try to grow their business. Sometimes even the first nickel went into the business. My friend and client Glenn Segal, a successful wholesaler, tells me that when he was just starting out, he and his bride slept on blankets on the floor, without a mattress—for a year—while he used any money he had to buy inventory for his business. You surely know the expression, "borrowing from Peter to pay Paul." In my own case, Paul was borrowing to pay Peter. (Peter was one of our executives: talented, but expensive.)

Insurance was a funding vehicle to help provide entrepreneurs with the liquidity that would be needed upon their deaths to pay estate taxes, to provide cash for their families, to buy out partners, to fund executive benefits, or to fund charitable bequests.

In 1978 Mark Solomon founded another company, then called the M Group, with his partner, Eli Morgan. Why M? There was Mark from Philadelphia, Pennsylvania, and Eli Morgan from Portland, Oregon. In a few years they teamed up with Carl Mammel from Omaha, Nebraska, then Peter Mullin from Los Angeles.

These four Ms were innovators to the nth degree. They created a new kind of company—the first buyers' co-op in the life insurance industry. This entrepreneurial experiment has grown to become one of our nation's premier financial-services design and product distribution companies. Here's how it came about.

The four Ms realized that successful entrepreneurs share several characteristics that they believed should reduce their life insurance costs:

- Successful entrepreneurs tend to take care of themselves physically. They tend to exercise regularly and get the best medical care available.

    Even in the 1970s, M clients ate healthy food, though periodically straying off the ranch (or onto it) for an excellent steak. The Ms thought that as a group, their clients' life expectancy should be better than that priced into traditional life insurance policies.

    The Ms thought that their clients should pay lower premiums for their life insurance, since the insurance companies should receive those premiums for a longer period. (Think of the premiums people would be willing to pay if insurers could guarantee that!)

- Because successful businesspeople tend to buy relatively large policies, economies of scale and technology should reduce the administrative cost of their insurance.

- Because both M clients and M producers are relatively sophisticated, the theory was that a better understanding of the transaction should lead to better persistency, the percentage of policies that do not lapse.

There's tremendous turnover in the traditional life insurance market, and one of the keys to profitability is persistency. The Ms thought this could be another cost advantage.

To phrase it another way, most people understand that to "win" as a life insurance policyholder—to collect the full benefit but pay few premiums—you need to die early. The good news is that most people in the United States are lucky enough *not* to die

50 | THE ETHICAL ENTREPRENEUR

50 | THE ETHICAL ENTREPRENEUR

early. The bad news is that most of them tire of the premiums, or can't afford to keep paying them. Thus, most folks' policies lapse before they do.

In the 1970s, the losses due to large numbers of lapsed policies was spread among all policyholders. The Ms were tired of subsidizing those lapses. The Ms felt that their clients would be happy to "lose" on this part of their portfolio by continuing to pay their insurance premiums for a long time—the longer, the better—until they died. This is an exception to a rule; in this case, the lower the internal rate of return, the better the investment.

One other factor proved significant. For these larger, more wholesale policies, the Ms were willing to accept lower up-front commissions compared with traditional retail policies.

Sharing the Rewards

The M producers agreed that we would put our money where our mouths were. Yes, we'd take lower commissions up front for selling the policies we helped create. But if we were successful, we wanted to share in the insurance company's long-term profits.

In exchange for the volume we believed we could deliver—along with superior mortality, superior persistency, lower administrative costs, and lower up-front commissions—we wanted to be partners. We wanted to share in future profits, if there were any.

Partners share risk. M producers not only wanted a piece of the upside; we were willing to participate in the downside. To this day, I am baffled by how many people only want to share in the ups—in the life insurance industry for sure, but in every industry and profession I know. Somebody's teaching something wrong, somewhere! Without risk, there just isn't entrepreneurship, and there just isn't any such thing as an upside without a downside.

Over the years, the M Group worked diligently with insurance companies and with an army of expensive but talented actuaries and attorneys to design and implement some fascinating mechanisms to share profits and losses. These esoteric formulas were sometimes too complicated for my taste, but they were effective.

The Ms also wanted a voice at the table. Those of us at CMS were pretty large producers. Yet to the insurance companies, our numbers were just a rounding error. The Ms thought that if they could team up with some other big producers, and corral enough buying power, we should be able to negotiate better economics, both for our clients and for ourselves. We weren't so naïve as to think we'd win every argument, but we figured that if we represented enough volume, we'd at least get the insurers' ears.[1]

The good news is that it worked.

The four Ms are to the life insurance industry what Bernie Marcus is to the home improvement industry and what John Bogle is to the mutual fund industry.

M, now known as M Financial, is based in Eli Morgan's original home city of Portland, and its longtime chair is Peter Mullin, from L.A. I wrote earlier about Paul borrowing to pay Peter. I can't begin to say how much wisdom and goodness I've borrowed from this particular Peter over the last forty years.

Now there are more than 140 M offices around the United States, Great Britain, and United Arab Emirates. Each is an independent insurance brokerage, investment firm and/or executive benefits company. CMS was one of the first. One of the more recent additions to M Financial is Rose Glen Advisors, organized by Morey Goldberg, who originally joined CMS in 1986.[2] Existing CMS life insurance policies are serviced by Rose Glen, and new life insurance prospects from the CMS network are often referred to Rose Glen.

Today, in the aggregate, M Financial's proprietary products represent more than $130 billion in death benefits, with cash values totaling nearly $40 billion. These policies are underwritten by insurers such as Prudential, John Hancock, Pacific Life, Lincoln Financial, TIAA, Unum, and ING, the successor to the original M carrier, Security Life of Denver. Today M Financial is the largest buyers' co-op in the insurance industry. If it were one of the 850-some life insurance companies in the United States, it would rank sixth in terms of new premiums.

Chapter 9

THE GOLDEN HORSESHOE

W hen Bernie Marcus was fired from his job as an executive at the Handy Dan Improvement Centers—at age forty-eight, with a wife, ex-wife, kids, and a mortgage—he called his investment banker and friend, Ken Langone, to tell him the bad news.

"No, no, you don't understand!" Ken insisted. "You've just been hit in the ass with a golden horseshoe." In *Built from Scratch*, Bernie and his co-author, Arthur Blank, tell the story of how an apparent calamity became the golden opportunity for the three of them to open a business of their own.[1]

Sometimes our biggest problems lead to our biggest opportunities. Of course, some of our biggest problems are of our own making. This is a story about how we at CMS almost hoisted ourselves on our own petard.

In the late 1970s and early 1980s we were grappling with a looming business problem. Life insurance is a tough product to sell. First, you're selling air, in the sense that it's an intangible. Second, you're selling lack of air, in the sense that you're selling death. We humans tend to have trouble putting our arms around a product we can't put our arms around. Link intangible with mortality, and you start to understand why the commissions are so high.

The biggest problem with pricing assumptions in life insurance is that assumptions are just assumptions. One assumption that you *can* safely make as a life insurance consumer is that you will die. The problem is that you just don't know when.

In addition to not knowing how long you'll live, you also won't know what kind of investment returns will be generated on the premiums you pay. If and when you find out whether the returns will be enough to sustain your policy, it may be too late!

Every actuary makes assumptions and predictions, but nobody can predict the ultimate result until either the train stops or you get off the train. Think about this in the context of a thirty, forty, or fifty-year life expectancy.

In 1979 interest rates were 11 percent. An aggressive company in California called Executive Life (which met its own well-deserved death in 1991) would provide you with an illustration that assumed that the 11 percent interest rate would continue for the rest of your life.

What would you do? Say your cousin-in-law wanted to sell you an $8 million Executive Life policy for a one-time premium of $100,000. Executive Life was at the time the largest life insurance company in California, and highly regarded by the ratings agencies.

Imagine that after your cousin-in-law's presentation, you then met another pushy insurance salesman (me) who told you this:

I have a better deal for you. I don't believe that interest rates will remain at 11 percent for forty years. I don't believe that Executive Life can deliver on the example they illustrate. Instead, if you want an $8 million death benefit until the day you die, which could be forty years or more, I recommend other large and highly rated insurers. However, I believe you should pay a single premium of $300,000 or $700,000—not the $100,000 suggested by the Executive Life agent.

If you're willing to assume the insurer will earn *and* credit you 8 percent every year for the next forty years, you should pay $300,000. If you're more comfortable assuming 6 percent per year for the next forty years, you should pay a single premium of $700,000.

One more thing: If you read the fine print of the Executive Life policy, you'll see that if the insurer earns and credits you with less than the assumed rate of 11 percent, you'll have to pay more premiums in the future if you want to maintain the $8 million death benefit. (If the insurer earns and credits more than the assumed rate, congratulations; your beneficiaries will receive more than $8 million as a death benefit.)

Given the choice, what would you do? For an $8 million death benefit, which single premium would you choose: $100,000, $300,000 or $700,000? Ah, the magic of compound interest—and the bliss of ignorance.

An Ethical Dilemma

This represents a classic dilemma that almost every entrepreneur will face sooner or later, regardless of industry or profession: Your competition will be selling b.s. Most of your potential customers won't ask the right questions and won't seek the right advice. If you're a salesperson, do you do the right thing—or do you go with the market and feed your kids?

Some folks argue that "professional salesman" is an oxymoron, that a salesman is biased by commissions. They say you should hire a consultant, pay a fee, and get objective advice. I say that those who say *that* are probably consultants. To me, it doesn't matter how someone is paid, whether by commissions or by fees. What matters are three things: Is that person ethical? A leader? An entrepreneur?

Lawyers are paid fees. If your lawyer is ethical, he or she may have one associate working your case, if that is what's called for. If your lawyer isn't ethical, he may have two associates billing you.

Even though I'm both a lawyer and an insurance salesman (heaven forbid!), I can claim objectivity because I've never practiced law and I no longer sell insurance. My #1 advice to any insurance buyer: Find a salesman *or* consultant who's ethical, and you'll probably get good advice. Advice #2: find a leader in the field—a salesman *or* consultant—and you'll probably get good advice. Advice #3: find an entrepreneur in the field—a salesman *or* consultant—and you'll probably get good advice. Bottom line: it matters less how the compensation is structured; what you need most is integrity *and* competency.

If your insurance salesperson or consultant is an entrepreneur, she or he has to attract and retain customers, and also needs to attract and retain employees. Good entrepreneurs are focused on the long term. Successful entrepreneurs should do the right thing, not only because it's the right thing to do but also because it's good business.

The principals of CMS and M Financial earned a reputation within the life insurance industry as leaders as well as ethical entrepreneurs. When we were asked—and even when we weren't asked—we'd advise clients that we didn't think Executive Life's illustrations were credible. We'd run illustrations from a whole host of insurers, with various interest-rate assumptions. We'd try to educate clients about the difference between gross and net. We'd point out the loads, both the insurer's and the producer's. We'd explain how, and when, a policy accumulated cash value. We'd question the guarantees. We'd question the assets behind the promises, and who was promising what, should both the insurer and the assets fail. We'd ask, "Why shouldn't you buy four $2 million policies from four different insurers instead of putting all your premium eggs in one $8 million basket?"

Compounding Executive Life's 11 percent compounding problem, the commissions on its policies were both high and front-loaded. You might be able to justify the commissions for an $800,000 policy, but not for an $8 million policy. Yet most states prohibited sales agents from giving policyholders rebates from the commissions, no matter how large the commissions might be.

A Plus and a Minus

To compete in a changing marketplace, someone at M invented a potent marketing tool called Plus Units, which turned out to pose some very interesting—and challenging—business issues.

Think of going to a buffet, choosing a little macaroni, some cheese, and maybe some broccoli to assuage the guilt. M Financial created a life insurance buffet. Plus Units were little pieces of non-commissionable life insurance that could be attached to your basic, commissionable policy. For example, if you chose to include 25 percent Plus Units in your policy, the commission would be only 75 percent of what it otherwise would be.

So why not choose 100 percent Plus Units, and pay zero commissions? Today you can buy no-load policies, and you can decide how much value you think your broker brings to the table, if any. I'd argue that there'd be no table if you didn't allow your broker to make a living. That was the essence of the dilemma over Plus Units. We pioneered the movement to levelized commissions. This provided higher early cash values to policy owners, which gave them greater flexibility. Levelized commissions also provided an ongoing revenue stream to the producer to help fund the ongoing service needs of the client.

The problem was that the more Plus Units we sold, the less we earned—so decreasing revenues against the increasing costs to properly service our clients could put us out of business.

Competition in the marketplace had knocked us sideways, and at first we weren't sure whether we'd been kicked by a horseshoe made of gold or one made of lead. But as we worked with our clients to strike a balance among the policies we sold, emphasizing our transparency as a competitive advantage, we were able to convert the problem into an opportunity.

Chapter 10

PLAY FAIR WITH
YOUR PARTNERS

As our clients' businesses grew, they started generating relatively large amounts of distributable cash. Some clients sold their businesses, which generated even more cash. This became a problem. Granted, having too much cash is a nice problem to have, but it can be a problem nonetheless.

We found that despite being terrific businesspeople, many of these entrepreneurs were terrible investors. They were consumed with their businesses, their families, their friends, and their community service. There just weren't enough hours in the day to do everything, so they didn't focus on their personal investments, certainly not relative to the amount of wealth they controlled. The proof was in the pudding.

My partners and I were tasting the same pudding—not quite as much pudding as our clients, but certainly enough. Our life insurance business was successful, but we were facing pressure on margins. And we were clueless about how to diversify our own personal investments.

In 1981 we launched an "investment club" called CMS Investment Resources. Through limited partnerships, which included fees, commissions, and profit participations, some of our clients pooled capital with us. We hired talented people to spend the time and to do the due diligence that neither our clients nor we were doing.

When we identified our first investment opportunity, a 128-unit garden apartment complex in Salem, New Jersey, we had to raise $300,000 in equity. At the time our intrepid sales force consisted primarily of Mark Solomon and me. There were a few other CMS'ers on the street, such as Bob Spivak and David Gerber, but they were then focused mostly on insurance sales.

I remember my first investment call. A few years before, in 1975, Mark and I had been introduced to Michael Kirschner by one of his lawyers. At that time Kirschner Brothers Oil Company owned gas stations in the Philadelphia/South Jersey area. The company had been founded in 1933 by two brothers, and in the mid-60s, Michael had joined the family business.[1]

The family had done some pretty sophisticated estate planning with their team, which included their attorneys, their accountants, and us. They bought some life insurance through CMS, and we developed a particularly close relationship with Michael. When I called Michael in 1981 to suggest that he consider investing with us in a garden apartment complex in Salem, New Jersey, he said, "I consider you and Mark two of the best insurance people in the United States. But what the f___ do you know about real estate?"

"Nothing," I replied, "but we're going to learn together."

Michael did invest in the Salem apartments, and in almost every other transaction we did for the next thirty-plus years. Some were pretty good; some were pretty awful. The one constant was trust. Michael anticipated then—and knows from experience now—that sometimes we'd be right and sometimes we'd be wrong, but we'd always try to do the right thing.

Aligning Our Interests

Trying to do the right thing included trying to align our clients' interests with our own in each and every CMS investment. We, the principals of CMS, put personal money—in amounts significant to our individual net worth—alongside Michael's and that of our other clients. We were limited partners on the same terms as our clients except that we didn't pay ourselves fees or commissions. That wouldn't have changed the economics to the clients but would have triggered an additional and unnecessary tax to us. We were also general partners. This is how we earned profit participation, if and when there was any.

Our profit participation ranged from 5 percent to 20 percent, typically after investors got back their original investment plus a preferred return. Depending on market conditions and a certain transaction's perceived risk, the "pref" was usually compounded in the range of 8 percent to 12 percent per annum.

We had a "no cherry-picking" rule whereby we prohibited ourselves from investing in any real estate or private equity, corporately or personally, unless we invited our clients to join us at the same time. We allowed two exceptions to this rule: One was for personal residences; the other was that each of us could personally invest up to $100,000 in a relative's or friend's transaction. This second exception was meant to allow us to demonstrate support, but on a scale small enough to avoid a meaningful conflict with our clients.

Sometimes we had more demand than supply. For example, a certain investment might require $10 million equity, whereas our clients (and we) wanted collectively to invest $20 million. CMS investors and their professionals knew the ground rules: Any member of the "club" who submitted documents by the closing date would participate. If we were oversubscribed, everyone (including ourselves) would receive a pro-rata participation such as 50 percent of the requested amount. Once the dust would settle on the amounts, we'd bill everybody for their pro-rata share, and then settle the accounts at closing.

People being people, some tried to game the system. A client who really wanted to invest $500,000 in a certain project might delay submitting his paperwork until the end of the offering period. He'd then request $1 million, anticipating that he'd end up with 50 percent—the $500,000 he wanted. Nobody said our clients weren't clever or entrepreneurial.

We were almost myopically focused on the ethics of the process. Over time we figured out a fairly effective way to bring parity to the table: We required clients to submit money along with their documents and warned them that they'd better be prepared to own what they asked for. We executed on our plan, and thereafter found very little "puffing" on the demand side.

Our policies were directly counter to the prevailing norms for investment firms. Many firms had a "first come, first served" protocol. Sometimes the starting times for the race to invest were staggered. Some firms would initially offer a hot investment to their best customers, then dole out leftovers to everyone else, if there were any.

While family is family, deadlines are deadlines. Every member of the CMS "family" could participate in a transaction as long as he or she responded by the designated date. You're welcome to call my wife, Aviva, to ask her how she was treated when she missed a deadline to get on the "Yes" list for an investment she wanted. That was a true test of ethics, and of my own courage!

Our attitude was that our investors were friends and clients, in that order. In the corporate world, "family" is a much overused—and much abused—term. I dare say, however, that if you were to poll CMS clients, partners, vendors, and employees, you'd often find the word "family" used to describe our firm. Over the years we did perform a number of such surveys, and oftentimes the word "family" was included in the responses.

Several years ago CMS decided to no longer create or market any new products. Nevertheless, until the value of the remaining real estate and private equity investments can be realized over the next several years, we're committed to bringing those investments to an appropriate conclusion for our family of clients.

As with any family, our CMS family has had plenty of dysfunction. But whenever a conflict arose, we tried to put our clients' interests ahead of our own.

Chapter 11
MAN PLANS, GOD LAUGHS

O
ne of CMS's first private equity investments (then called leveraged buyouts, or LBOs), was participation in Thomas H. Lee's first fund, in the mid-1980s. Our partnership was the second-largest investor in Lee's fund, after Prudential. We then invested in Lee's second fund, which had a few terrible investments, but nobody noticed because that portfolio also included a company called Snapple. Two and a half years later, when Tom and his partners sold Snapple—for a return on equity of 30x—everyone was happy. This success made a strong case for diversification, and at CMS we started thinking about other ways to apply the lesson.

For CMS, financial planning seemed like a natural progression from our specialty in life insurance and estate planning, so we opened a new division called Capital Management Systems (again, CMS). We tracked participating clients' assets, and their sources and uses of funds. We spent a lot of time trying to help clients understand and articulate their objectives as well as any special issues.

We worked closely with our clients, their families, their accountants, their lawyers, and their other professionals to help create comprehensive financial plans. We offered asset-allocation advice, a manager-of-managers service for stocks and bonds, and alternative investments in real estate, private equity, hedge funds (the latter two were then cottage industries), and, of course, life insurance.

As we better understood each client's needs, we were also better able to understand the aggregate needs of the group. This gave us the confidence to negotiate access to investments that were being marketed to large institutional buyers and were not otherwise available to individuals, even those with high net worth.

CMS had one additional differentiator for our "club:" successful entrepreneurs accessing other successful entrepreneurs. For example, when we, or one of the outside investors to whom we wanted access, had questions about a person or product in a particular industry, often our relationships were able to provide due diligence information that proved valuable.

That model worked well for a number of years. Then, during the next decade, in the 1990s, financial planning became commoditized. All sorts of people started calling themselves "financial planners." Some sold advice—estate planning, asset allocation, manager selection. Some sold product—life insurance, stocks and bonds, hedge funds, real estate, leveraged buyouts. Some sold all of those. Regardless, they all called themselves financial planners.

We felt we no longer offered a unique product or service. To make matters worse, as a "manager of managers" we were picking the pickers of stocks and bonds, but in those traditional liquid markets our returns, net of fees, were worse than if we'd invested in passive index funds. Why hadn't we met John Bogle back then?

I'll never forget Bernie Marcus's admonition to us: "Guys, I like you very much. I don't want to fire you, but you're putting our whole relationship at risk."

A lot of our other clients agreed with Bernie. Not only were we risking client relationships, but that part of our business wasn't even profitable—a bad combination. So we fired ourselves.

We weaned ourselves out of stocks and bonds by giving that business to our managers. They became the managers of the manager of managers! Those clients who liked the service kept it and weren't burdened with the taxes or administrative headaches normally associated with a change of accounts.

In retrospect I regret abandoning that business because I think our clients, and ourselves, would have been better off if we'd kept it and fixed it. Fixing the performance would have meant transitioning from active managers to passive index funds. That could have also fixed the profitability problem, which we subsequently could have compounded with greater volume. Twenty-five years ago, when we exited this business, we had about $1.4 billion in stocks and bonds under management. If we had fixed it, and stuck with it, my guess is that by now we'd have $20 billion under management, maybe more. Oh well. . . .

Most people say, "Stick to your knitting," and they're usually right. We were life insurance people. We didn't do so well with stocks and bonds. On the other hand, if we had stuck to our core business, we wouldn't have invested in Snapple or in garden apartments.

Some folks ask if I became bored by having the same job for almost fifty years. To the contrary, I was addicted to my business, as are most entrepreneurs. For the most part, I enjoyed it immensely, mainly because of the long-term relationships, and because we kept reinventing ourselves. On the other hand, the years during and following the Great Recession weren't so much fun.

Exploring Alternatives

During our first decade, the 1970s, our business at CMS was exclusively life insurance. In the 1980s we focused on financial planning; in the 1990s, alternative investments. Structurally speaking, we offered three types of alternative investments: access, co-invest, and direct.

Our access funds did just that: We accessed other funds, and we created "funds of funds" to invest in several different LBO funds within a single CMS fund. The advantage of a fund of funds was that it offered additional diversification; the disadvantage was additional fees.

For funds of funds our clients paid a "double promote," since they paid fees to the underlying fund managers and also to CMS. This led to our second category, called co-investments. We, and other institutional-type investors, would negotiate co-investments with leveraged buyout managers. In exchange for CMS raising $X for their funds, at full fees, we acquired the right to invest $Y directly into some of their portfolio companies. Since the fund managers didn't charge fees on the co-investments, our clients paid a single fee (to CMS).

Our third type of alternative investing was "direct." In the private equity world, CMS's sweet spot was buying companies with revenues from $10 million to $100 million and earnings from $2 million to $5 million. We would try to buy from 70 percent to 90 percent of the company; management would typically own the remaining shares. We tried to buy at a valuation of four or five times EBITDA (earnings before interest, taxes, depreciation, and amortization).

Where possible, we used our network to help improve operations and drive growth in the companies we owned. We called these investments management buyouts (MBOs), as opposed to leveraged buyouts (LBOs). LBOs were famous for their focus on leverage and financial engineering. Our MBO emphasis was on management and operations. Just semantics? We didn't think so.

We also were active in both access investing and direct investing in real estate. Our most successful real estate niche was buying Class B garden apartment complexes, primarily in the Southeastern United States. These properties usually included 200 to 400 apartment units, requiring equity investments in the range of $5 million to $10 million. We liked to pay 10x to 12x cash flow; today the market is 14x to 18x. Over the years CMS partnerships acquired (and subsequently sold) about 60,000 apartment units.

By the late 1990s, a huge amount of institutional money was chasing all kinds of alternative investments. The big buyers were driving prices sky high. We found it impossible to buy at prices with which we were comfortable, so we became sellers. By the time the Great Recession hit in 2008, we had reduced our equity under management from $3.5 billion to $1.1 billion.

For our fourth decade, the 2000s, we decided that smaller is better, except for our insurance business, where we believed the opposite. In our real estate and private equity investing, we sharpened our focus on direct investing. We had been raising about $400 million equity per year, with our business plan headed to $600 million. But as the saying goes, "Man planned, God laughed." Driven by constraints on the supply of what we considered compelling investment opportunities, we reduced our target raise to $150 million per annum.

The good news was two-fold. We sold assets at a good time, and I believe our shift in strategy was prudent. The bad news was also two-fold: The 2000-era funds were too small to create meaningful profits from the fees, and then the recession hit, so we weren't able to create profits from asset sales.

The toughest part was downsizing the various companies, from 120 employees to eighty in 2001, then to forty in 2008. The industry called it "rightsizing," but there was no right side to it.

When I had to lay off dozens of employees, I couldn't sleep. It was devastating to have to deliver the terrible news, and it's still very painful to think of so many of our loyal employees and their families who had to not only receive that news but then live with it.

After the Great Recession we recognized that our best-laid plans had failed, and we had to focus on two things: trying to protect our clients, and trying to survive in business.

Chapter 12

BIG WALLET, BIG HEART, HOME FOR DINNER

W hen it comes to consultants I'm a bit of a hypocrite. On the one hand, I find myself biased against them. On the other hand, I can't imagine where I'd be without them. And in many ways, I am one!

When CMS decided to launch an investment business in 1981, our biggest challenge was to find good investments. Our second biggest challenge was to persuade our clients that we were no longer just in the life insurance business.

Early on, we met two management consultants from Southern California, Alan Boal and Terry White, who called their company Idea Transfer. Their name turned out to be true to its promise: They did indeed transfer their ideas to us, and we in turn successfully transferred our ideas to our clients. These ideas transformed our companies, and I'll bet these ideas, modified to fit your own entrepreneurial bent, can help you build your own companies.

The Ideal Client System

Alan and Terry taught us how to use a process they called the Ideal Client System. The Ideal Client System is a step-by-step path to a successful business relationship. It begins at your very first eye contact with a prospect, and it should culminate in a strong relationship based on understanding, positive experiences, and trust. A client who is comfortably and enthusiastically referring his or her peers to you has become your Ideal Client.

The Ideal Client System has six stages:[1]

Stage 1. First Impression. You only get one first—of anything. The first impression you create sets the stage for your marketing. Your first impression will be lasting; you have sixty seconds to make it a good one.

"Since you never get a second chance," said Alan Boal, "you'd better take it seriously. Write down your First Impression script. Memorize it. Practice it. Make your employees memorize it. Make them practice it." We at CMS created—and re-created, and re-created—our First Impression Script. We practiced it, and practiced it, and practiced it.

This first stage may be short or it may be an extended process. My partner Bill Landman and I once travelled two and a half hours, each way, for a First Impression meeting that lasted ten minutes. That prospect became one of our best clients.

Following our first meeting with a prospect, and following *every* subsequent meeting, we'd recap the information delivered and lay the groundwork for our next meeting. We called these Action Letters, and our protocol called for an Action Letter to be sent within forty-eight hours of a meeting. An Action Letter kept the client focused and also kept the CMS team focused on what was important to the client, what the next steps should be, and who should take them.

Stage 2. Discovery. Long-term business relationships are built on the capacity to identify multiple client needs, clarify expectations, and implement solutions with integrity. This requires a willingness to listen, to understand, and to demonstrate the ability to represent the client in a highly professional manner. Discovery is fact-finding. It's also the time to position value and to build trust.

This stage sometimes requires a great deal of patience; I once pursued a prospect in the Discovery stage for ten years. Obviously, my first impression hadn't been as good as I'd hoped. On the tenth anniversary of my pursuit, I sent this prospect an email: "We should touch base once every ten years, whether we need to or not!" My persistence won the day. We subsequently built a very meaningful relationship.

Stage 3. Trial. Here's the area where we were really screwing up, and our consultants were worth every nickel we paid them for their advice.

Even before we began working with Idea Transfer, we were pretty good at First Impression and Discovery. But then we'd rush back to the office, enlist far too many people, run far too many illustrations, and prepare far too formal a proposal. The proposal would be far too complicated and far too thick.

CMS spent a fortune creating these presentations. When we'd present one of these beauts, we'd get to page two (out of 102), and the prospect would say: "You assumed my business is growing at 5 percent per year. Cheap imports are killing my margins. I'm looking at negative growth."

Oops. Also facing negative growth were CMS margins, as well as our credibility. Idea Transfer taught us that we were jumping from Discovery to Decision without allowing time for discussion, reflection, and modification of our proposals. We needed a process of Trial.

Trial is all about concepts and round numbers on the back of an envelope. It lets prospects sample what you do and how you think. It lets you design a plan for the client *with* the client. It allows you to test and confirm assumptions.

Trial is a valuable opportunity to incorporate other professionals into the process. It's a unique chance to make preliminary decisions in an informal setting and to learn how the client prefers to be presented with information and decisions.

During this stage, designing a plan for ongoing service creates positive expectations and reinforces mutual commitment to a long-term relationship. This further reduces the client's anxiety and allows for decisive, affirmative action.

Stage 4. Decision. The concept is presented during the Trial stage; the "Yes" is obtained in the Decision stage.

How do you help your client to become informed and comfortable with the value of your products and services? You must reduce anxiety; educate; design the service side of the relationship; and define expectations.

Clients feel most comfortable when they are presented with a clear, concise summary of their needs. This allows them to easily review alternative solutions and the associated risk versus rewards. Idea Transfer encouraged us to be the ones to raise any natural questions or objections. This allowed us to position ourselves as thorough fiduciaries.

Our clients were perceptive, skeptical, and funny. I told one client that I viewed myself as a buyer on his behalf, and asked him to consider joining me in one of the CMS investments. He said to me, "For a buyer, you're a pretty good seller!"

Information is the basis of a logical decision. Reduce anxiety by helping your client to become an informed buyer. Present information concisely in several courses, not all at once. Never make a prospective client feel intimidated by your understanding of the subject matter. Use layman's terms, without patronizing.

Stage 5. Commitment. The driving force behind any successful client relationship is service.

For this stage, the objectives are to complete the transaction; to avoid creating buyer's remorse; to convert service into repeat business and profitable relationships; to enhance the reputation of your services and your products; and to obtain referrals.

Providing ongoing service reassures clients that they have made the right decision. Proactive service and communication will further cement the relationship and create new opportunities: Your client may not be aware of other services that you provide; you may discover that the client has additional needs; and by serving your client's needs, you position your firm for active referrals, and, even more potent, for spontaneous blessings when one of their friends inquires about you.

Stage 6. The Ideal Client. After credibility, your most important asset is a base of satisfied clients. Existing clients have the greatest access to, and credibility with, ideal prospects.

Clients are much more likely to make referrals when they know what to say. Idea Transfer taught us how to position our best clients—our Ideal Clients—as unofficial members of CMS's board. We asked our Ideal Clients for input on CMS's policies, its positioning statement, its client profile, and its credo. With this familiarity they could then define appropriate business opportunities and communicate the potential value necessary to arrange introductory meetings.

The Ideal Client system allowed us to leverage existing client relationships and to create an active source of new business. Clients became CMS emissaries, which allowed us to devote less attention to marketing and more time and energy to product and service.

We designed all sorts of codes to maintain information about our clients in our computerized tracking system. A client who was actively making referrals was an A-6, meaning an Active Client in Stage 6. Our first A-6 was Michael Kirschner. (He was the one who had questioned our grasp of real estate when we first entered that market.)

Mark Solomon and I met Michael in 1975, and two years later he joined Mark on a mission to Israel. Every Friday night since then—for forty years and counting—I get a phone call from Michael: "Shabbat Shalom." (That's Hebrew for "May you have a peaceful Sabbath.") The Jewish Sabbath starts at sundown on Friday, and considering that both of us tend to travel a lot, sometimes it's a challenge to figure out the time zones for the phone call.

The Ideal Entrepreneur

A lot of people were active in life insurance, real estate, and private equity. How did we differentiate ourselves? A lawyer in Boston told us, "What people want to know is: (1) with whom you work; (2) what makes you unique; and (3) what you do. And in that order!" He was 100 percent correct.

Our client focus was the successful entrepreneur. That in itself separated us from the crowd. Most insurance and investment folks would talk with anybody who would talk with them, particularly if they had some money. We were laser-focused, trying to network only to entrepreneurs.

Why limit our client base when there were a lot of wealthy folks out there—doctors, lawyers, athletes, entertainers, beneficiaries of inheritances? First, we enjoyed spending time with entrepreneurs. Second, entrepreneurs generated deal flow for our investment company. Third, as industry leaders, these highly successful entrepreneurs helped us in our due diligence. Fourth, they helped us maximize value in our good investments and fix problems in our bad ones.

Entrepreneurs were ideal clients for us because they understood risk. And among the things that made our company attractive to them was its narrow client focus; there was a feeling of exclusivity to the club concept, and the "negative sell" is powerful.

We defined entrepreneur very broadly, but with three qualifiers: big wallet; big heart; home for dinner.

Big Wallet. When we launched our investment company we sought clients who were earning at least $175,000 a year. As we grew, we ultimately looked for prospects who could invest at least $5 million in illiquid assets and/or generate $100,000 in life insurance commissions. Yes, some of our clients had bigger wallets—and some smaller. (We helped some to get bigger, and, unfortunately, some to get smaller!)

Big Heart. We looked for shared values. We chose to hang out with good businesspeople who did good things with their money.

It drove us nuts when we met people who, despite their tremendous wealth, didn't share it with the community. Some of our employees thought that we were insane to turn down financially qualified prospects, but we believed that shared values meant better clients. We thought that when we hit troubled waters, they wouldn't jump ship; we thought they'd give us time to try to resolve a problem rather than just call their lawyer. It turned out to be true.

Home for Dinner. We sought clients within a three-hour commute of Philadelphia. New York City and Washington, D.C., were easy, and we also had clients in Boston, Chicago, and Atlanta, where we had a shot at getting home for dinner. When a call came from Los Angeles or Las Vegas, we were flattered and tempted, but we usually said, "Thank you, but no thank you."

In any business, trust is everything. The Ideal Client System creates clients and it creates trust.

The only way to earn trust is by uncompromisingly doing the right thing. When people trust you, they will buy your products and services and refer others to do the same. Often it's not the quickest buck, or the easiest. But it's the best buck you can earn.

Chapter 13
DO THE RIGHT THING

S ome people claim that philanthropy is a private matter that has no place in the business world. I disagree, and thousands of years of law and traditions in many cultures teach us differently. The philosopher Maimonides said that anonymous giving is only mandated between the donor and the recipient, so as not to embarrass the recipient; otherwise, you should make an example of yourself when you give.

The best fighting force in the world is reputed to be the Israel Defense Forces. Israel's survival depends on it. Its leadership mantra is *Acharai*, which in Hebrew means "Follow me." So be it for leadership in *any* endeavor. This includes entrepreneurship. It includes philanthropy.

Are there ever tensions between ethics and money-making? Of course. What in life doesn't require some tradeoffs? Doing the right thing often requires a longer time horizon. It often requires a larger upfront investment: money, yes, but also blood, sweat, and tears.

But doing the right thing ultimately pays, fiscally as well as psychically. It seems so self-evident that I just don't understand why more entrepreneurs don't make it their first priority to do the right thing.

Sometimes we're tested.

In 1997 our investment company raised $50 million in equity for a fund to invest in collateralized loan obligations (CLOs). All of us had worked for months on this transaction, and a consortium of Wall Street firms had raised $500 million for the debt. The money was sitting in an escrow account at a bank. The closing was scheduled for a Wednesday.

On Monday night my partner Bill Landman called an emergency meeting of the CMS principals. Bill said, "My team and I have lost confidence in this manager. We're afraid that he can't deliver what he's promising. I know it's the eleventh hour, but I don't think we should proceed with the transaction."[1]

The next morning we cancelled our offering and returned to our clients all $50 million, including our fees.

The Wall Street firms went crazy. Several of their investment bankers told us, "Nobody ever does this! We earned our fees. Put the money to work. When the clients earn less than they anticipate, you can blame it on the market. That's the way it works."[2]

One of the investors in this transaction was Bernie Marcus. When Mark Solomon and I next saw him, he literally stood up and applauded: "You should do this every two or three years," he said. "Just collect some money from me, put it in escrow, and return it a couple months later. It makes me a believer all over again!"

The More You Give, the More You Get

Even in the late 1980s, when we first met him, Bernie Marcus was exceptionally wealthy: Wealthy in dollars and cents; wealthy in common sense; most importantly, wealthy in his sense of values. If you know Bernie, or if you read his book, *Built from Scratch,* you'll know that he was exceptionally smart—and exceptionally values-driven—from early childhood.

Early in our relationship Bernie came to Philadelphia to check us out, and he's visited our company several times since. Here's an excerpt from a talk he gave to the CMS staff on September 13, 1995, when he was still very much in charge of The Home Depot:

My mother had a saying that the more you give, the more you get. So it became a selfish kind of thing. In other words, if you did something for somebody else, you would then get more back. This is what she taught me.

You have a credo. Our credo is very close to your credo. Our credo is that the customer is our life. The customer is the reason for our existence. The customer eventually will give us the things that we want out of life.

Tomorrow I'll go to Toronto. I'll be walking five stores; I'll be wearing an orange apron. I will have with me district managers, merchandisers, the people from Chicago, Toronto, etcetera. Tomorrow night we'll have dinner. And I'll say, "It's your agenda. Tell me what you want to discuss. No holds barred. Everybody has immunity. You can say anything you want. Tell us how stupid we are; tell us what we are doing wrong. It is very important that we listen to you and hear what we are doing wrong." They make up an agenda. Typically it is fifty to sixty items. On Friday, I will spend the day going through every single item.

After Toronto, I have two days of training. I will give the last class. The class will last eight hours, and in that time I will explain our philosophy, our way of doing business. One of the points I make is that we believe in people. We want people treated with dignity. We feel very strongly that our lives are interwoven: that this is a family, even though it is 79,000 people. We will tell them that they are disciples. They have to go back to the stores and carry the message, because the culture is the thing that makes The Home Depot so different.

Part of that culture is what we do for the community. Nobody needs to tell our people what to do. They know how we feel. When the FBI needed to have a certain light bulb because they were working through the night after the Oklahoma City bombing, we woke the people up at GE, and had them fly it in. We set up a portable shower for the firemen on the scene, with a hot water heater. I never told them to do that. Nobody told them.

We have a thing called Team Depot. Every single store in the chain is involved in something in their community, building ramps for the disabled, whatever. And they do it on their own time. We supply the material. You think about what that does for the fabric of a company. This is part of the cement that runs through the whole of the company.

What does this have to do with CMS?

I am very careful about who I do business with. It took me many, many years to accumulate what I have. I must hear ten schemes a day. People who call me up and say, "You have to do this." I'll say, "Why?" They'll say, "Because you will make a lot of money; I'll make you rich." I'll say, "I'm rich already. Tell me why I should invest with you? The truth is, you want me to invest with you because you'll get rich. That's really your purpose. Isn't that right?"

There are two things that impressed me about Mark Solomon. The first thing was that he invests in every deal in which he was asking me to invest. A major consideration. The second one came up later, and that was his involvement in the community.

When somebody has as their basis a very strong philanthropic thread that runs through their being, it is a strength. This is the basis of a good character. You show me somebody who is very, very charitable, and who is a thief, and I'll show you somebody who is unique and

unusual. You don't usually find thieves who are charitable
and share with others.[3]

A Failure to Act

Whenever I've neglected to act on my convictions, I've regretted it.

One of these regrets concerns my lack of leadership on an incident regarding CMS's Charity Plan. In the mid-nineties, nineteen of our employees participated in a plan to share any profits that might be generated from our successful investments. To participate in the upside, however, an employee also was required to participate in the CMS Charity Plan. All participants, including the company's principals, contributed a percentage of their gross earnings, "off the top," to the CMS Foundation. Contributions started at a modest percentage and progressed up to 10 percent.

Half of each employee's charitable contribution went into a corporate pot from which we gave collectively to various philanthropies in the name of CMS. The other half of the contribution was deposited in each participant's personal account, and the CMS Foundation sent checks to whatever charities the participant selected, in the employee's name. CMS either withheld the agreed-upon contribution from participants' paychecks, or the employees would make an annual contribution from their bonus or from appreciated stock.

When one of our managers told us that he was experiencing a personal cash crunch, we agreed to temporarily defer his contributions, and during the next couple of years we contributed

$67,000 to the foundation in his name as a loan to be repaid out of future bonuses. We were diligent in documenting the repayment plan, and we were diligent in our communication to the manager.

The problem was that he refused to repay the loan. He also wanted us to pay him 100 percent of his own targeted bonus.

I felt we should fire him. The manager of this manager made excuses for him and prevailed on our executive committee, which I happened to chair, not to terminate his employment. I acquiesced.

To this day I resent the manager's lack of integrity, and I blame myself for not having the courage of my convictions. Though I believe that integrity is non-negotiable, in this instance I negotiated it. That was a big mistake. It was the wrong lesson to the manager. It was the wrong lesson to our other employees. It was the wrong lesson to my partners. It was the wrong lesson to my soul.

The Golden Rule

Because the principals of CMS were social activists for decades, many people regarded the company as a role model. On the one hand I was proud of that, but I was also frustrated that we were considered an exception. Why? Hadn't our churches, temples, and mosques taught us, for thousands of years, to integrate community service—and ethics—into our businesses?

Thirty-three years ago I was introduced to a kindred spirit, Victor Hammel, who had just begun running his family business, J.C. Ehrlich Company, which was then a modest pest-control company based in Reading, Pennsylvania. Under Vic's leadership the company flourished while taking as its working principle the German meaning of the family name: "honest."

Recently Vic told me that years ago, when his father, Simon Ehrlich Hammel, called on customers in Pennsylvania's German communities, he would often tell them, in German, that they were dealing with an Ehrlich man—an honorable, honest man—and the customers would smile, but they also would feel reassured. But during the Watergate scandal of the 1970s, when President Nixon's aide, John Ehrlichman, was sent to prison for conspiracy and obstruction of justice, it was a very sad time for Simon Ehrlich Hammel.

During his years leading the company, Vic opened each training session with these words:

"Do unto others as you would have them do unto you"—The Golden Rule:

Hinduism, 3200 BC, "One should always treat others as they themselves wish to be treated."

Judaism, 1300 BC, "Thou shalt love thy neighbor as thyself."

Buddhism, 560 BC, "Hurt not others with that which pains yourself."

Confucianism, 557 BC, "What you do not want done to yourself, do not do to others."

Christianity, 30 AD, "Whatsoever ye would that others should do to you, do ye even so to them."

Islam, 570 AD, "No one of you is a believer until he loves for his neighbor what he loves for himself."[4]

"Ethics is like your skin," Vic says. "It goes with you everywhere. Ethics is a moral perspective that asks you to judge your conduct in terms of what's right and wrong, what's good, what's honorable. The reason to be ethical is simply that it's the right thing to do."

Vic valued his coworkers even above his customers, recognizing that he could not have satisfied customers without a satisfied workforce. "Ethics are good for business," he says. "Companies with a reputation for ethical behavior attract more and better job applicants, result in a higher-caliber work force, retain coworkers longer, and grow and prosper more."

When Vic did some research to compare the most ethically admired companies with other publicly owned companies, he found that the average annual growth rate of companies rated "most ethical" was nearly double that of the others.

His conclusion: "In business, ethics is about behavior. Not about a person's goodness. Not about religious beliefs. Not about philosophy. It is about applying ethics to daily decisions."

Sweet Success

You'll find that the ancient philosophy of the Golden Rule guides the leaders of many other successful businesses. Two of those whom I admire share several other qualities: Each has developed an international clientele, each has roots in Toronto, and both have brought a great deal of pleasure to their clients.

One of these businesses has been recognized every year for the last eighteen years on *Fortune*'s list of the "100 Best Companies to Work For:" the Four Seasons Hotels and Resorts. The company was founded by Isadore ("Issy") Sharp, the Canadian son of Polish immigrants who became known to the company's employees as a frequent visitor to his properties, walking the hotels and meeting with management.

One clue to the corporate culture he established can be found by reading how his wife, Rosalie, described him in the foreword to his book, *Four Seasons: The Story of a Business Philosophy* (which any aspiring entrepreneur should read):

. . . . Trust and integrity have been the foundation of Four Seasons. Issy was a leader with no notion of the prescribed tenets of how to run a company, and no MBA.

He made a lot of brash decisions—against the trends and pundits' advice—stubbornly trusting in intuition.

Issy has an almost zealous code of social commandments and believes that ethics is the religion that unites and motivates his people.

"The only thing you can control,'" Isadore says, "is your attitude."[5]

Sandra L. ("Sandy") Solmon is an entrepreneur who shares Issy Sharp's outlook. Sandy grew up in Toronto and graduated from the University of California at Berkeley. She could have stayed at Berkeley and become a flower child, but instead she moved to the town of Reading in Southeastern Pennsylvania. "I had to do something," she said, "so I started baking cookies."[6]

She started by setting up a baking operation in a garage and selling her cookies to local convenience stores. Her first nine employees belonged to an ashram; she would meditate with them on their work breaks. Today, if you enjoy a cupcake or a brownie in Ulan Bator, Mongolia, or at a café in any of sixty other countries, there's a good chance that it was made by some of Sandy's 700 employees in Reading. Sandy grew Sweet Street Desserts to become the world's largest gourmet dessert company.

I met Sandy some thirty years ago, when we were both in our thirties. At that time she was one of the few women members of our local Young Presidents' Organization (YPO). I was not a very active member of our chapter, but I did attend the annual ski trip and I did show up for my monthly forum meetings, where I met Sandy.

The YPO forum was a gathering of peers who gave an oath of confidentiality in order to encourage candid conversations about business, family, and community. The eleven men in our group would be frustrated when this one woman would show up late, but she always won us over with her sheepish smile, warm heart, and wickedly delicious new desserts. She always brought samples of her newest concoctions: Tartiness trumped tardiness.

Sandy's creativity has been recognized with her industry's highest honor, Cornell University's Hospitality Innovator Award. Always passionate in her quest for her next breakthrough, Sandy now says, "The market is finally catching up to me. I'll be the first to have GMO-free, cage-free eggs, sustainable chocolates, no artificial flavors, no trans-fats, no corn syrup, no hormones in dairy."

She's also created a corporate culture that counts integrity among its essential ingredients. In her company's mission statement she puts it like this:

"Sweet Street is about more than great food. Above all, we are dedicated to creating a safe, dynamic and gratifying environment so compelling, our customers, suppliers, and co-workers want to participate in achieving mutual success. By continuing to conduct ourselves with the utmost integrity and by anticipating the best interest of these valued people, our company's sweet success is certain."

Sandy has been a committed champion of community for the thirty years I've known her. If you're a big fish in any pond you're recruited to join all sorts of community boards, and Sandy wanted to make a difference, but she wanted to do it in another way.

Some of Sandy's comments really hit home with me:

"Life is like wandering on a river," she said. "Unexpectedly you're in the rapids. Then you end up going down one tributary, purely by accident, which changes your life, or changes how you perceive your life.

"This happened to me about ten or twelve years ago, when I kissed a pig. The Boys and Girls Club of Reading holds an annual 'kiss a pig' fundraising campaign. When it was my turn, I finally understood the difference between active and passive giving. I understood what the Bill Gates of the world are trying to do.

"Doing the right thing was so ingrained in me, from my mom, that I just did it. Then I started wandering down another tributary."

One day her stepfather called to talk about one of his friends, a neurosurgeon in Southern California who was focused on stem cell research for Parkinson's Disease. Sandy recalls that her stepfather believed that his friend wanted leadership for his lab, and he also believed that if Sandy helped him, she could make a contribution while creating a promising new business.

"I got excited," Sandy recalls. "I thought, this could really make a difference." The outcome was that Sandy became CEO and lead venture investor of Celavie Biosciences, Inc., a company dedicated to developing treatments and a cure for Parkinson's Disease.

"It's now ten years and $15 million later," Sandy says. "I keep investing in it because it's something I believe in. This is a tributary story that has impacted and overwhelmed my life."

I asked, "Are you hoping to save the world, or make $1 billion?"

"Both," said Sandy.[7]

Here's a literal example of having your cake and eating it too: Sandy's passion to do good *and* do well has created significant rewards for herself, for her family, and for her community.

A Competitive Advantage

My tenure at CMS confirms that there is no conflict between doing the right thing and doing business. Doing the right thing *is* good for business. We at CMS served the community, and the community served CMS. New hires at CMS often commented that our commitment to community service was the leading motivator in their desire to join CMS.

CMS's community activism was also important to our clients. Everyone in the financial services industry wanted to do business with our clients because they were leaders in their industries as well as in their communities. Why did these leaders want to do business with CMS? We asked many of them that question many times over many years, and most responded by citing the company's reputation for integrity and community service.

Are values a substitute for performance? Of course not. But our clients told us that product and service were not enough. They required integrity, and they preferred to do business with people who gave back to the community. CMS's mission for almost half a century had been to create wealth for clients, for the community, and for CMS, and in that order.

One of our responsibilities as principals of the firm was to teach those values to our own employees. Each year we closed for a Day of Caring when all of us worked together on a project such as rehabbing an inner-city child-care center, and many of our associates, myself included, mentored students from disadvantaged neighborhoods as part of the Big Brother/Big Sister program. CMS employees contributed to the United Way and for years were recognized for making the biggest per-capita gifts in Philadelphia. One of our employees initiated the CMS Turkey-a-Thon, which provided hundreds of Thanksgiving meals for homeless families each year. I could go on.

As of late there's been a tsunami of publicity about corporate philanthropy, often as part of branding and marketing strategies. Many of these programs lack authenticity, and my skepticism is reinforced when I hear about inefficiency, theft, and other forms of corruption within corporations as well as charitable organizations. On the other hand, I believe in mixed motives and don't mind when the right thing is done for the wrong reason. I applaud the results when they produce a positive outcome.

The idea that one can separate personal values from business values is anathema to me. Is ethical entrepreneurship an oxymoron? Absolutely not!

And it's not complicated. John Bogle puts it this way: "As Vanguard got big, our manual became huge, but it boils down to: Do what's right."[8]

To be a true leader, you need to be authentic, and you need to follow the Golden Rule that has been an essential principle in so many cultures for thousands of years. These stories demonstrate a clear correlation between ethics and successful entrepreneurship: Bread cast upon the waters ultimately comes back as loaves.

Chapter 14
ACHARAI: FOLLOW ME!

I f you believe in giving back—by investing your time, your energy, and your money in good causes—you probably find yourself in the position of having to ask others to do the same.

From the first days of my career in 1969, I spent most of my time trying to persuade people to buy things from me. I've also spent a significant amount of my time asking friends, clients, colleagues, and strangers to give away their money.

In analyzing the common denominators that have contributed to the success of various campaigns I have led, I've boiled them down to ten strategies that I call my Ten Campaign Commandments. They're not carved in stone, and you'll need to make your own modifications as appropriate to your campaigns.

101

These are my Ten Campaign Commandments:

1. Define your mission.
There are always competing missions and pressure from different constituencies: Don't diffuse your message.

In 1998 the mission for Philadelphia's Tocqueville Society campaign was to double its membership. The Tocqueville Society is United Way's leadership giving category, which consists of donors of $10,000 or more each year. At that time, among the country's fifty-six major cities, Philadelphia was ranked fifty-sixth. The City of Brotherly Love might have been the best in love, but we were the worst in giving.

The legendary Philadelphia entrepreneur Pete Musser, founder of Safeguard Scientifics, joined me in this campaign as co-chair. Some of the United Way leadership wanted our campaign to focus on increasing the giving levels of existing donors. While this is important in any campaign, I feel strongly that one of the reasons for our dramatic success was our focus on one mission: to expand the base. Everything else was secondary. Future campaigns could focus on increasing giving levels, but our job was to double membership in the Tocqueville Society.

In that campaign, our marketing theme was "Leaders lead." Not that needs aren't important—but how do you sell the needs of 250 agencies? Our Tocqueville story was that Philadelphia's United Way campaign had hit bottom, and it was time for our business leaders to rally. It worked: Over our three-year campaign we grew our Society from 124 members to 333, and Philadelphia raised its ranking from #56 to #1 in the United States.

2. Remember that people give to people.

People respond to crises. People respond to opportunities. But most important, people respond to people!

All of us are solicited, all the time, for all kinds of charities. I have yet to be asked to give to a bad cause. So how do you differentiate your cause? First, by who asks.

Your solicitation is an endorsement of that organization. You transfer your credibility; you vouch for its effectiveness. You spend some of your very valuable and very finite relationship capital.

A word of caution if you're campaigning for the first time: Fundraising is an expensive avocation. As a solicitor, not only must you have made your own leadership gift, but it is only a matter of time before those you solicit approach you for their own causes. Reciprocity need not be dollar for dollar, but it adds up.

3. Define your impact.

All of us want to make an impact. If you are running a crisis campaign, be careful not to cry wolf. If you are running an opportunity campaign, rally around a glorious vision to make a difference.

An example of a glorious opportunity campaign was the $80 million "Built to Last" campaign I chaired for Yemin Orde, a residential school in Israel that rescues orphans and at-risk children from twenty-two countries around the world and helps them to become productive citizens and effective leaders. The dazzling vision of our "Built to Last" campaign, which lasted nine years, from 1999 to 2008, was that we were literally saving lives while at the same time having the potential to impact Israel's entire residential education system. Speak about leverage!

4. Go public with your goal.

Set your goal and set it high: doable, but high. Make it dramatic. Dream big—it's the American way! It's not the dollar amount that counts; it's what you're going to accomplish.

Then take the next step: Go public with your goal. Once you and your leadership commit publicly to the goal, it can become a self-fulfilling prophecy. But make sure you have your lead gifts lined up before you go public, so as to lend credibility to the campaign.

Best efforts do not work. Going public with your goal can be a somewhat risky proposition. It can be embarrassing if you fall short of the goal, and maybe even costly.

During the first Intifada in 1989, when nobody was traveling to Israel, I co-chaired the first "mega-mission" in the United States: We chartered two El Al 747s to depart (for the first time ever) from Philadelphia to Tel Aviv. We called it MISSION 1000. Up to that time the largest mission our community had sent to Israel was 200 people, and that was during peacetime. A thousand people during a war?

Most folks thought we were crazy. In fact, my partner Mark Solomon called me one night and said, "Paul, we sold out the first plane. This in itself is a miracle. Our Federation now has to pay for the second plane, which costs $330,000 whether it flies with one *toochis* in it or 440. Since we won't let the Federation get stuck, you and I will have to pay for the unused seats. Call it a victory. Let's go back to work."

My response: "That's exactly why we need to commit to the second plane. If we commit, we'll sell it." And we did.

Remember, your goal will become the ceiling, so be aggressive.

5. Assign bite-size tasks.

Break your goal into small pieces. Assuming your goal is set high enough, there is probably no way you are going to accomplish it by yourself. If you want to run a campaign for individual donors, my suggestion is to recruit a campaign cabinet of thirty or forty solicitors.

I call this the Rule of Thirds: In every campaign I have run, one-third of our cabinet really produced; one-third did a little bit; and one-third did absolutely nothing. The interesting thing is that I have never been able to predict which solicitor would end up in which column. If you recruit a thirty-person cabinet, you'll end up with ten real workers. If you start with a cabinet of only ten people, the entire burden will be on your shoulders plus one or two others.

In recruiting your cabinet, ask each member for only a few very specific, bite-size tasks. For example, ask he or she to attend one and only one organizational meeting (people resent meetings on top of meetings), and to solicit only one gift per month for five months. You're asking very busy people for a small amount of their time, but to accomplish very important tasks.

6. Establish deadlines and send report cards.

All of us need deadlines. We are competing against all kinds of priorities, so be sure to establish deadlines throughout your campaign. For example, if you reach half your goal halfway into the campaign, emphasize that you only have so many months to finish the job. Use the deadline to propel the campaign by creating a self-imposed crisis.

One of the most important strategies, but the one most often omitted, is to reinforce deadlines by communicating heavily with your cabinet. Once a month, send a report card to each cabinet member with a column for each month of the campaign and a list of successful solicitations by each member of the cabinet. Every month you should fill in the amount of each successful solicitation, and the donor's name, together with the name of the solicitor.

Make sure that you and a few other zealots conclude some successful solicitations prior to mailing the first report card so that it reflects momentum. With so many demands on our time, campaign calls are often deferred despite our best intentions. But when you know that a report card is going out to your peers, those calls tend to rise to the top of the to-do list. We are motivated to show our peers that we live up to our commitments.

7. Cultivate your lists.

Update your donor list and send it out regularly to your cabinet. But also periodically send the donor list to all donors, and to all prospects. Actively manage your prospect list. Periodically ask members of your cabinet as well as *all* donors to help identify additional qualified prospects.

While the purpose of an extensive direct mail campaign is to sensitize people to be more receptive when they are personally solicited, an unintended result in every campaign I have run is a surprising number of "mail order" gifts.

8. Establish a challenge gift.

Though they're becoming a little over-used, challenge gifts are still among the most effective tools for fundraising. Donors like the 2:1 leverage.

9. Focus on friend-raising.

A successful campaign is a relationship campaign. Ideally you want to forge an ongoing and growing relationship between the donor and your organization. So first focus on friend-raising.

For example, to raise money for the youth village of Yemin Orde we organized trips to Israel that included on-site visits to the village; its Executive Director Chaim Peri and other key personnel periodically visited friends of Yemin Orde in the States; every couple of years we brought a choir of a dozen Yemin Orde children to tour the States; and Chaim sent a very moving letter each quarter to update friends on happenings at the village, both good news and bad.

Think of a naming opportunity as the beginning of a relationship. Naming opportunities work, and they should be plentiful. But don't take the gift, attach the plaque, and think you're done. Maintain dialogue with that donor about his or her project. Personalize it. Send photos. Ask the children, or whoever uses the facility or the program, to write letters to the donors. Do whatever you can to enhance the donor's feelings of ownership and pride.

And as long as you're going to ask for a gift, why not ask for that same amount payable each year for the next five years? You won't always get what you ask for, but you'll be surprised how often you do. Multiple-year gifts are efficient, since you don't have to ask again next year and the next. They provide a terrific base to build on each subsequent year. They help build ongoing relationships because the donor is committed for five years—*but* be sure to keep the donor engaged. What could be better than going back to the donor each year to enhance friend-raising, with no pressure to ask each time for another gift? On the other hand, what could be worse than ignoring the donor for five years and then knocking on the door with your tin cup?

10. Just ask!

In every campaign I've run during almost five decades, the single most important reason for our success was simply that we asked.

In his book *Mega Gifts* Jerold Panas writes, "Many tenets are important, but the greatest of these is: You must ask for the gift. This may appear to be overly fundamental, but too often this cardinal principle is overlooked. The tongue gets heavy and thick, the hands perspire. But every salesperson knows that finally, inevitably—you must ask for the order. This is the greatest commandment of all."[1]

Successful campaigners spell *NO* with a "G"—as *GO*. Every "No" gets you closer to the next "Yes." With patience and perseverance, you can often turn "No" into "Yes."

If you take a deep breath and let yourself be guided by these ten commandments, you will have a successful campaign. While it will be a lot of hard work, and frustrating at times for sure, you can significantly leverage your philanthropy, make a real impact, and at the same time have a lot of fun.

Chapter 15

UP THE SLIPPERY SLOPE

Of the hundreds of articles and books I've read while researching the topic of ethical entrepreneurship, the most disturbing—and yet the most hopeful—is a short article published in 2014 by the Harvard Business Review titled "How Unethical Behavior Becomes Habit" by Francesca Gino, Lisa D. Ordóñez, and David Welsh.

This article so upset me that I can't tell you how many times I've distributed it, quoted it, debated it, re-read it, hoped I was reading it wrong, and hoped the authors were wrong!

Here's what they had to say:

. . . . Bernie Madoff commented to his own secretary, "Well, you know what happens is, it starts out with you taking a little bit. . . . You get comfortable with that, and before you know it, it snowballs into something big."

Many of the biggest business scandals of recent years . . . have followed a similar pattern: The ethical behavior of those involved eroded over time.

. . . . We all are vulnerable to the same slippery slope. We are likely to begin with small indiscretions such as taking home office supplies, exaggerating mileage statements, or miscategorizing a personal meal in a restaurant as business-related.

Nearly three-quarters of the employees who responded to one survey reported that they had observed unethical or illegal behavior by coworkers in the past year.[1]

That last sentence is devastating.

Is it human nature to "round up?" Does rationalizing minor indiscretions inevitably lead to bigger offenses?

The authors continue:

To make matters worse, people are more likely to overlook the unethical behavior of others when it deteriorates gradually over time. . . . Unfortunately, the assumption that unethical workplace behavior is the product of a few bad apples has blinded many organizations to the fact that we all can be negatively influenced by situational forces, even when we care a great deal about honesty. [2]

Here's the good news: The authors of this article credit the book *Nudge: Improving Decisions about Health, Wealth, and Happiness*, whose authors, Richard Thaler and Cass Sunstein, have observed that an unobtrusive nudge in the right direction can help people make better choices. In their own research, Gino, Ordóñez, and Welsh have also found that "ethical nudges can help people avoid the types of indiscretions that might start them down the slippery slope."

Despite their finding that unethical behavior can become habit, the authors of this study also offer this message of hope for any leader who aspires to inspire:

Environments that nudge employees in the right direction, and managers who immediately identify and address problems, can stop ethical breaches before they spiral out of control.[3]

For better and for worse, each manager is a messenger—one who teaches bad habits that can spread like a disease, sapping the spirit of a company and eroding its values, or someone who sets a standard that lifts everyone up.

At CMS we were fortunate that for many years our Vice President of Human Resources was Trish Peirce. One of her most difficult responsibilities was to help me and our executive committee plan and execute a significant downsizing in 2001. She then had to do it again, in 2008. What made a horrible situation even worse was that Trish's position also became obsolescent in 2008. She knew it; we all knew it. The Great Recession displaced a lot of good people, and Trish was one of the best. (One lucky— and smart—company subsequently hired her, and both benefited.)

Over the years I've stayed in touch with Trish, and while I was working on the manuscript for this book I sent her some samples, asking for her thoughts, and she sent this gracious reply:

How much better would we all be if more people heard these messages in their everyday life? You brought these messages into every important event at CMS that I can remember.

. . . . I recall one time when I had a personal issue. I can still see your face when you told me, "You need to be where you are needed most." I think of that time any time I waver about choosing a family priority over a work priority. I use that same message to any one of the twenty people who now report to me, as I see them struggling to balance work and family commitments. You made me a great manager! [4]

Her recollection confirms that a positive message, no matter how small, can become a nudge in the right direction that impacts a life.

Every entrepreneur is a messenger who sets out a direction for others to follow—on a path that leads down the slippery slope, or upward.

Chapter 16

THE BUSINESS OF FAMILY

I 'd like to tell you two stories about two twentysomethings. They both spent their teens in a relatively large, beautiful suburban home. They travelled extensively and enjoyed family vacations in luxury resorts around the world. They were not immune to the volatility of the teen years, nor to the negative influences that often travel with affluence. I marvel at how grounded they are. On the other hand, I'm not very objective when it comes to these two young ladies. After all, they're my daughters.

I could write volumes about each one of them. For now, I'll tell just one story about each.

As I've described, I met my Israeli spouse in Israel—as did both of our daughters. I met Aviva in her parents' home in Jerusalem, over a cup of coffee. Both our daughters met their spouses in Tel Aviv bars, over mugs of beer. Maybe it's in their DNA?

When I visited our older daughter, Tamar, in Israel, just after she moved in with her boyfriend, I thought I would have a heart attack. The apartment was so small that the refrigerator was outside, on the porch. The mattress was on the floor and took up the entire bedroom. Her boyfriend, Yoav Shiffman, was a university student, fully supporting himself by bartending at night and working in strawberry fields during the day. He rented a tiny apartment on a kibbutz north of Tel Aviv, surrounded by his strawberry fields and an army of tiny ants, humongous beetles, and all kinds of many-legged creatures.

I was appalled, but at the same time I was thrilled. Tamar was genuinely happy. Aviva and I were so pleased that money and differing lifestyles hadn't gotten in the way of love. Once we got to know Yoav, we were particularly proud (though not surprised) to see that Tamar had chosen a mate with values quite similar to those we had tried to impress upon her.

Our younger daughter, Tali, gave us angst from the day she was born, three months before her due date. You need to be a fighter to survive at 2.2 pounds, especially in 1984, when technology wasn't what it is today. Tali is a fighter. As a preemie, she fought—and she frightened us, and as a teenager she fought us—and frightened us. (Many teenagers feel that's their job!)

But Aviva and I always knew that the fight was well worth it. Five years ago, we dropped Tali at the airport to embark on her *aliyah*: She was moving to Israel to make a life there with a young attorney, Yoni Abadi, whom she'd met in a Tel Aviv bar. When Aviva and I returned home we each found a letter from her. Mine said in part:

———

Dear Daddy,

You taught me never to fear change or what lies ahead, but to step forward with grace and dignity, and know that the morals and values that are inside will guide me in the right direction.

You have always been there, through the joyous times and the hard times. I want to thank you for being there for me, supporting me in everything I do (yes, I know it's a lot of different things, and they sometimes contradict, like social work and shopping), and most of all, for being you. I pray that Yoni will be a dad just like you.

———

How can I begin to count my blessings? I have so many more; it often doesn't seem fair that I have so many. Two of my blessings are my daughters. Two more of my blessings are my sons-in-law. You can't imagine how many times I've asked each of my daughters, "Do you appreciate how special and unique are your husbands?" (And I've also beseeched them, "Please, please, please try not to screw it up!")

Tamar's Yoav and Tali's Yoni are true *menschim*. (That's Hebrew for "good persons." If you want to give a Jewish person the highest compliment you can, just call him or her a *mensch*.)

Of course, it takes one to know one, and my sons-in-law acknowledge that they, too, are fortunate that their respective spouses said "Yes."

I think the two lessons learned here are these: If you're single and looking for a mate, don't compromise on values; and if you're having trouble finding the right one, try a Tel Aviv bar!

Set an Agenda

Chance meetings have changed my own life, too.

One day long before my daughters were born, a number of people were relaxing on one of Nassau's beautiful beaches, doing what people normally do on a beach—except for two men who were sitting on the beach with families in tow and their briefcases open, work in hand. Toronto's Michael Shulman introduced himself to Philadelphia's Mark Solomon, and they became good friends. A year or so later, when I went to work for Mark Solomon in 1971, I was fortunate to also be adopted by Michael Shulman, who's helped mentor me to this day.

Michael headed the largest entrepreneurial accounting firm in Canada. Then, about twenty years ago, he decided to cut back his work to twenty hours a week and to launch his own consulting firm. Over the years he limited his consulting practice to six families at any given time. These clients needed to satisfy the same criteria that CMS set for its own business: His clients needed a big wallet to pay his healthy retainer; they needed to have a big heart—shared values—to qualify for this "club;" and they needed to be Toronto-based so that Michael could be home for dinner with his family.[1]

When our daughters were in that frisky teenage stage, I decided that I needed a family consultant. I couldn't afford Michael's fees, and I wasn't Toronto-based, but Michael and I shared values, and because I was one of Michael's adoptees he gave me the gift of his consulting services. It isn't necessarily true that you get what you pay for; in this case, no fee could have paid for the value that Michael transmitted to me and my family. With his permission I used his agenda almost verbatim for our first family meeting on April 26, 2000. Since then I've forwarded it to countless others, and with Michael's permission I've included it here for your own use as Appendix 2.

When Aviva and I arranged our first family meeting, our daughters were sixteen and eighteen. If you have daughters or sons who are ready, I suggest that you do as I did and make good use of Michael's work. Otherwise, don't lose this agenda; it's timeless, and when the time comes you'll find that it's priceless.

Over the years the agendas for our family meetings evolved, but they always included the basics: integrity; relationships; budgeting; investment philosophy and asset allocation; and philanthropic philosophy and allocation to *tzedakah* (Hebrew for "obligation" or "justice;" there is no translation to "charity"). At our second family meeting Aviva and I set a monthly personal allowance for each daughter and an annual allowance for charitable gifts. Tamar and Tali were each given an annual stipend of $1,800 for charity; they had to research and report to the family as to which organizations they wanted to allocate that money.

Aviva and I always circulated proposed agendas in advance, and we also solicited questions for discussion from family advisors and occasional guest speakers as well as from the standing participants. The four of us eventually became the six of us after an appropriate "probationary" period for Tamar's and Tali's spouses. Some advisors advise against including in-laws in family financial meetings, recognizing a divorce rate higher than 50 percent. I'm in the full disclosure camp, but I also believe in prenuptial agreements and irrevocable lifetime trusts.

Our notes from those meetings suggest some of the questions we regularly discuss:

- You only live once: Spend vs save? Safety net vs lifestyle? Our next gen vs your next gen?
- Investments: Diversification vs concentration? Allocation vs market timing? Preserve vs grow? Expertise vs fees and aligned interests? Passive vs active?
- Philanthropy: Measuring impact, relationships/anecdotal vs metrics? Communal vs starfish? Costs vs clean hands? Due diligence vs time? Focus vs diversification? Mission creep vs "change creates opportunity"? Institutions vs individuals?
- Flexibility: As per the IDF (Israel Defense Forces), this battle plan is good till the first shot is fired!

We've had some fascinating and fun discussions, and some of the most valuable lessons are ones that Aviva and I have learned from the younger generation.

At our family meeting two years ago Aviva and I announced that we intended to continue to own one of our family-held real estate assets, but sell another. At that time I had been in the real estate business for thirty-three years and Yoav had been in the real estate business for six. I presented my case. Yoav took the opposite view and presented his case. A heated discussion ensued. His case was better than my case, and the family unanimously decided to sell the one I had planned to hold and to hold the one I had planned to sell. In retrospect, I believe the advice from the next generation, and the discussion it engendered, produced a better result.

Your Three Beneficiaries

Estate planning is both complicated and simple.

In 1977 The Brookings Institution published a treatise by George Cooper which is still in print called *A Voluntary Tax? New Perspectives on Sophisticated Estate Tax Avoidance.* He quoted testimony to a Congressional committee: "In fact, we haven't got an estate tax, what we have, you pay an estate tax if you want to; if you don't want to, you don't have to."[2]

George Cooper, who was then a professor of law at Columbia University, and his wife, Judy Blume, the author of bestselling children's books, happened to have a vacation home on Martha's Vineyard, where they were friends and neighbors of Mark Solomon. When his report was published, CMS purchased a few hundred reprints, and we used those reprints to help educate clients (and their professionals) on estate planning techniques, and to help us sell a lot of insurance.

Cooper's 1977 treatise has circulated through Congress for nearly forty years. Over that period of time, Congress has legislated away almost every technique for estate tax avoidance that he exposed—our government doesn't work quickly, but better late than never, I suppose.

In lieu of many of the tax avoidance schemes exposed by George Cooper, many of our clients, and we ourselves, took a much simpler approach to estate planning by implementing what we called The Community Plan.

The provisions of the estate tax system are terribly complex, but its basic outlines are extremely simple. The simple version is that, in round numbers, estates (or gifts during a lifetime) that exceed $10 million are taxed at 50 percent at the second death of husband and wife. That's a tax on what's left after an income tax of 50 percent (less for capital gains), rounding up to account for state taxes and other costs.

For example, let's say that you're a good leader and an ethical, successful entrepreneur who earns $100 million. In the simplistic version, you pay in round numbers $50 million in income taxes. Assume you and your spouse then die. Ignoring exemptions and exclusions, your kids pay a 50 percent estate tax, and they have $25 million left. When your kids die, your grandkids will pay another estate tax of another 50 percent, and your grandchildren will then have $12.5 million left.

To recap: Of your $100 million in earnings, Uncle Sam gets $87.5 million, your kids get $25 million, and your grandkids ultimately inherit $12.5 million.

Many years ago CMS began to promote what we called The Community Plan. To continue the example, let's concede the $50 million income tax on your $100 million earnings, so at death your "gross estate" will be $50 million. You have two kids, and you decide that you want each one to inherit a safety net in the amount of $5 million, for a total of $10 million. You set up a trust and transfer assets to the trust over time, using various techniques to mitigate the gift tax that would otherwise be 50 percent.

Next, let's say that your trust buys a $10 million policy on your life (or a joint policy insuring both you and your spouse, payable at the second death). Assume you arrange to transfer the premiums for that policy to the trust over time, and that between premiums and gift taxes and other expenses, the total cost to the trust to buy $10 million insurance is $5 million. Everything else that's left in your estate you bequeath to charity.

When you die, your children will have the use of the $10 million in the trust. It's not the $25 million they otherwise would've inherited, *but* it's the amount that *you* decided is the right amount.

When your kids die, your grandchildren also will have the use of the $10 million in the trust, to the extent that it hasn't been consumed by their parents. This compares to the $12.5 million which they would otherwise have inherited under the "do nothing" plan.

You can determine whether you want your grandkids to inherit the money outright or continue the trusts for another generation. There are non-financial reasons for continuing trusts: divorce; second husbands who become lawyers; bankruptcy. The tradeoffs are flexibility and costs.

I have two other non-financial recommendations. Regardless of the size of your estate, if you don't yet have a good lawyer, you should find one and write a will. Early is better; you can change your mind and write new wills as circumstances change. If you have few assets and no children, a will is simple and inexpensive but can save a lot of unnecessary costs. If you do have children, you should decide what will happen to them if something should happen to you.

To recap the example of estate planning, under The Community Plan, of your $100 million earnings, Uncle Sam gets $50 million from income taxes but zero from estate taxes. Of your $50 million estate, Uncle Sam gets zero, your children get $10 million, and charity gets $45 million (in this example, the $10 million policy costs $5 million).

Estate planning is essentially simple because at the end of the day you have only three possible beneficiaries: family, community, and government. All fancy estate planning is just a conglomerate of techniques to allocate your wealth among these three beneficiaries. In this $100 million example, for the second generation:

No plan: Family=$12.5 million; Charity=$00.0; IRS=$87.5 million.

With plan: Family=$10.0 million; Charity=$45.0 million; IRS=$50.0 million.

(The extra $5 million is the leverage of good estate tax planning and life insurance.)

We at CMS helped our clients to redirect billions of dollars of assets from the federal government to charitable organizations.

Was that the ethical thing to do?

Was that effective entrepreneurship?

The waste and inefficiency of the federal government is well documented. But evidence of fraud and corruption within charitable organizations is also pervasive. Which beneficiary is more deserving of your earnings?

Chapter 17

JUST BE THERE

One of my company's essential criteria for accepting new clients was clear-cut: Home for dinner. The idea was to make sure that our clients' locations would allow us to spend our evenings with our families, aside from one or two nights a week for business travel or philanthropy. But in the years when we were building the company, the concept turned out to be difficult to execute.

Aviva and I have different memories of that period. I like to think that I recognized, early in my career, that many of my peers were one-dimensionally focused on their business. They spent too little time with their children, and it showed. I remember deciding that most nights I would be home for dinner with my girls.

Whatever my good intentions, Aviva recalls a different scenario. She says that I was on the same all-business track as some of my peers, heading for a family train wreck. One evening around midnight when I tried to sneak into bed without waking her, Aviva warned me: "If you keep working at this insane pace, I'm telling you that one night when you come home, the kids and I will not be here. I'm not willing to live my life this way."

I will never forget those words. And I did change my behavior.

Then came the issue of weekends. I was still logging way too many hours at the office when Aviva "gently" suggested that I should be with the family on the Jewish Sabbath, from sundown Friday through sundown Saturday. That, too, turned out to be a good idea. To be ecumenical, I also stopped going to the office on Sundays. To try to keep up with my work I usually started my day at four a.m., before the kids woke. (I still haven't been able to break that habit. It's productive, but at times exhausting.)

Transitioning from a work schedule of 24/7 to 14/5 was an amazing experience. I'm convinced that not only did it save my marriage and my health, but it also made me a better businessperson.

A Game Changer

Our family began to embrace a nice tradition whereby Saturdays became one-on-one days. I'd be with daughter Tamar one Saturday while Aviva was with daughter Tali, then vice-versa the next Saturday. The four of us spent Sundays together.

During the work week I usually could control my own schedule. I showed up at just about every one of my daughters' basketball games, softball games, five a.m. skating lessons—you name it—and one incident helped to convince me that just being there really meant something.

Some of the games were almost painful to watch; Jewish day school basketball isn't exactly the NBA. To attend one game I traveled about an hour to the middle of nowhere to watch one of Tamar's away games. The home team was well represented with parents and other locals, but in this rather large arena I was the single fan on the visitors' side, rooting for the fearless Akiba Cougars.

I kept my eye on the clock. An executive committee meeting was scheduled back at the office, and I knew I'd be fighting traffic. When the game went into overtime, I was beside myself. As the Cougars huddled, I put on my coat, hoping I could exit unobtrusively; hadn't I paid my dues? Then, from the huddle, Tamar caught my eye and signaled, "Daddy, just five more minutes." I called the office and told them to start without me. The next five minutes were very long—but gratifying.

Often it's the little things that people always remember, because their impact can be huge.

In 1965 I left home to start college at the University of Pennsylvania. My home was a small town in North Jersey, where my Dad had a busy dental practice and where he volunteered for the West Caldwell Borough Council and a host of other organizations.

One night, on the telephone, my Dad asked, "Sonny Boy, what's wrong?" He heard it in my voice. "Nothing. Really. I just didn't get an invitation to the fraternity I wanted. No big deal."

While it's a little embarrassing to think back about it, at the time it was a big deal to me. I was feeling rejected, dejected, and despondent.

Without saying a word to me, the next day my Dad cancelled his appointments and just showed up in Philly. We spent a few hours together, and then he drove home. Philadelphia was only a hundred miles away, but it took a full day to travel back and forth. To this day, a tear wells up when I think how important that emotional hug was to me at such a vulnerable time.

My Uninvited Visitor

Many years later, in 1982, I was introduced to a prospect, Robert Schwartz, who had assumed leadership of a small family-owned nutritional food supplement business called Food Sciences Corporation, which he was building into a large, national company. Robert and I established a nice rapport and a casual business relationship.

Two years later Aviva and I had a family crisis when our second daughter, Tali, was born three months prematurely. We were terrified. All of a sudden our world was turned upside down. We didn't know if our "tiny dew drop" (one English translation for the Hebrew name *Tali*) even had a "prayer" (the other translation). For three months Tali remained in the hospital's Neonatal Intensive Care Unit (NICU), and Aviva wouldn't leave her for more than a few minutes. During those three months I juggled my time doing three things: spending as much time as possible with our two-year-old daughter, Tamar; visiting Tali and Aviva; and trying to take care of business at the office. Fortunately, Aviva's mom flew in from Israel to help us (although we almost lost her at JFK Airport because she had no knowledge of English and cell phones weren't nearly as common at that time).

We didn't know whether Tali was going to live her life on a machine or even if she would survive. We were heartbroken.

No visitors were allowed in the NICU, but two outsiders habitually broke this rule. They scrubbed and gowned and sneaked upstairs to visit us and to support us. One was my partner, Mark Solomon. His presence was much appreciated, although, knowing Mark, not a surprise.

The other perpetual "illegal" NICU visitor was this almost total stranger, my new client, Robert Schwartz. He also began to show up at our home, insisting on babysitting our two-year-old so that I could go to the hospital to visit Aviva and our two-pounder. Aviva's mom would come with me and take Aviva out for a break. Robert would also show up at my office—uninvited, unannounced—and gently force me to take walks with him, to break the tension, to talk, to cry. Who was this crazy guy? He was everywhere. He was relentless. At the time I had no idea how much I needed him.

Three decades later, Tali is a wonderfully healthy woman who has so far awarded Aviva and me with two spectacular grandchildren. To this day Robert is ever-present in my life. For both, I say "Thank God."

Even when I question whether or not there is a God, I still take a few moments each morning to say thanks. My belief is that it's not only the duty of an ethical entrepreneur, but also an honor, to appreciate and to be thankful for what we have. Whether or not you say thanks to a higher power, that's your business. But hey, what's the downside?

I try to practice Robert's lesson whenever the opportunity presents itself. Pre-Robert, I would hesitate to show up when people I knew had a crisis. "Maybe they want privacy," I'd say to myself. "I don't know them that well. It's not really appropriate to impose myself." Post-Robert, I just show up.

What did I learn from Dad's post-fraternity rejection hug? From Tamar's glance through her overtime huddle? From Robert's ever-presence during Tali's fight for life? People may not know what they want during periods of emotional stress, but they do need support, and they will long appreciate your kindness.

These are the lessons that my family, my friends, and my colleagues have taught me, in my personal life and in my professional life:

Don't hesitate; just be there.

Relationships are almost everything.

Everything else is your name.

With a good name, you'll earn more. And you'll yearn less.

CONCLUSION

Sometimes I think I'm going crazy—along with the rest of the world. I just can't comprehend man's relentless inhumanity to man.

The lack of ethics in so many parts of our lives is appalling, and corporate corruption is blatant. Every day we hear about a new scandal of profiteering or malicious negligence that causes injury or death: exploding airbags in passenger cars; price-gouging by manufacturers of lifesaving drugs; bribery to government officials by chemical companies to avoid bans on toxic chemicals; and even within the medical profession, where unscrupulous physicians make fortunes by performing unnecessary surgeries and administering expensive, deadly chemotherapies to patients who don't have cancer.

Yet I remain an optimist.

The stories of the many honest entrepreneurs I know give me hope, and I recognize that those who quietly maintain high ethical standards seldom generate headlines.

I like to keep in mind my shoe salesman's advice. Ken Sherman is a second-generation entrepreneur in a family business whose reputation for quality and service has made Sherman Brothers shoe stores an institution in the Philadelphia area. Ken puts it like this: "The sign of a *mensch* is to do the right thing when nobody's looking."

I'm sure you know many a *mensch*—Jewish, Christian, and Muslim—who share a commitment to doing the right thing and a responsibility for making the world a better place.

Only through our individual actions can we hope to repair the world and earn peace of mind. In Hebrew this concept is called *tikkun olam*. One way to work toward implementing this concept is to set a simple goal: To be able to put your head on your pillow each night and know that you did one thing that day to help others.

For nearly fifty years I've prominently displayed in my office a quotation from the philosopher Hillel. Anyone who aspires to succeed in becoming an ethical entrepreneur needs only these words as a guide:

If I am not for myself, who will be for me?
And if I am only for myself, what am I?
And if not now, when?

Appendix 1
THE CMS CREDO

Our Mission. We focus all of our energies on helping entrepreneurs grow, manage, and preserve wealth for the benefit of their families and their communities. While our products and services may change from time to time, nothing will change the underpinnings of our business—that of providing an unusually high level of due diligence on products, services, and ideas for the successful entrepreneur.

Our Business Philosophy. We want to be known as a high-performance, high-integrity group of people who make a difference. Yes, making money is important, but helping our clients meet their objectives is more important. Our philosophy is that if we help our clients, we will be rewarded. Maybe not today, but someday we will be compensated. Stated simply, we are in the relationship business.

We will only recommend products and services which we believe to be the best available. We operate on the theory that one day our papers will be graded. On that day, the most knowledgeable person on the subject is going to walk in and our work will be laid bare. Our recommendations must be capable of withstanding this test.

We prefer to under-promise and over-perform. While this may cost us some business in the short run, it will guarantee our long-term success. Every time we deliver more than expected the bond between ourselves and our clients is strengthened.

Our Responsibility. Second in importance only to helping our clients meet their objectives is making this a better world than we found it. We, as a firm, are committed to helping others who are less fortunate than ourselves to develop their full potential. This means that all CMSers have a responsibility to put something back. We believe there are two kinds of people in the world, miners and farmers. Miners only take out; farmers take out but also put something back. We only want to be associated with farmers.

Our Primary Asset. Our greatest asset is our credibility. A client must be able to take our word to the bank. White lies or misrepresentations are unacceptable. Mistakes, however, are acceptable as long as we own up to them. The only people who do not make mistakes are those who do not make decisions.

Our Investment Policy. Unlike other firms, no transaction for investment purposes is retained by CMS for the exclusive benefit of its principals. To the contrary, all investments are made available to clients. Partners are required to invest in all CMS transactions and, except for a $100,000 exemption, are not allowed to make outside investments in asset classes in which CMS is then active.

Our Commitment. We are committed to doing "whatever it takes" to serve our clients. These are not just buzz words; they express the very essence of CMS.

Appendix 2
AGENDA FOR A
FIRST FAMILY MEETING

As described in Chapter 16, Toronto's Michael Shulman generously guided us in planning our family's initial meeting and provided us with an agenda which we followed nearly word for word. He also has allowed us to share our version of it here.

TO: TAMAR AND TALI SILBERBERG
FROM: PAUL AND AVIVA SILBERBERG
DATE: APRIL 26, 2000
RE: INITIAL FAMILY MEETING

I. Purpose of the Meeting

To inform and educate you about our family asset base and the basic values and strategies underlying and surrounding these assets.

II. Why have we chosen to do this with you?

- Someday, whatever is left after we are gone will be yours and the community's. You should be knowledgeable about the assets so that you can make better-informed decisions.
- One or both of you will have to manage the assets for your own interests, or perhaps for us if we can't do it due to ill health.
- Your interests are to trust each other, respect each other, communicate well, and be smart and grow the assets.
- Respect the assets. We've spent our lives developing them, and we want you to enjoy what we hope will be the growing rewards. The growing rewards will be up to the two of you.

This is the first family meeting. There will be more if you so wish.

III. Our Fundamental Goals

- To maintain and enhance our family harmony.
- To maintain and enhance our capital asset base.
- To maintain and enhance a good quality of life.
- To give back to the community.
- To maintain our individual privacy.

Family members must have financial independence in order to lead their lives without other family members interfering and being judgmental.

An important factor in families owning assets together is that each member of the family should have an independent career to provide income for daily living and independence. This will also free up the family investment assets to grow, and allow increased charitable giving.

IV. Our Strategies
- Our strategy has been to develop a broad basket of investments. Diversification is key (eggs into other baskets), such as:
  A. Liquid Assets
     Cash
     Bonds
     Stocks
  B. Illiquid Assets (CMS)
     Real estate
     Private equity (operating businesses)
     Alternative investments (structured products, hedging strategies)
- We do not believe in borrowing, as we never want to be controlled by a creditor (bank). Also, high borrowing can get you into trouble when recessions come. Borrowing is acceptable against a specific asset where there is no recourse to us personally.

- We believe in getting the best talent as managers and partners. Invest in people, not transactions. There is no such thing as a good investment with bad people.

V. Partner Relationships

- All our investments with partners, including CMS, are governed by legal partner/shareholder agreements.

    Typical clauses are voting for decisions; how do you get out of the investment; the obligations and rights of the partners.

    In the future, if you are to own assets together, it will be important for you to have clear understandings on these types of issues and to create your own written agreement as well.

- Investment decisions require:
    Careful study
    Evaluation of the risk factors
    Good people judgment
    Development and maintenance of excellent partner relationships of integrity.
    Tax planning
    Identification of good professional advisors

VI. Legal Structures

- Any assets which may be owned by trusts or corporations for the benefit of the children, although legally yours, are morally for the benefit of parents while we are alive.

- Trusts are often used to reduce or avoid estate taxes; otherwise the government would ultimately take 50 percent to 80 percent of the value of the estate for taxes.

VII. Charity

- Our family makes current gifts through the CMS Endowment Foundation.
- Ultimate giving will be through our family foundation. You will be trustees and should allocate our money according to what you believe would be our desires. (When you earn your own money, you of course will give it away in any way you choose.)

VIII. Expectations

- Our self-imposed obligation is to provide you with a good quality of life, the cost of productive education, and a financial safety net to cover emergencies/contingencies.
- After your education is finished, your expectations from these assets should be zero, for the following reasons:

    The best investments and the best quality assets can, unfortunately, disappear in bad times.

    It's impossible to avoid and insulate oneself totally from potential lawsuits, which can wipe out assets.

    The assets, either in whole or in part, may be given away.

    The assets may be used up for the parents' quality of life during our lifetimes.

IX. Michael Shulman's Six Traits of Healthy Families

- A positive attitude to life.
- Closeness and independence are a consequence of love.
- Parents make decisions with full family consultation.
- Communication is open, direct, and thorough.
- Everyone is realistic and practical.
- Everyone adapts well to change.

Appendix 3
LETTERS TO MY FAMILY

I f you've read this far, you know how important my family is to me. The values that we hold, and the love that we share, endure from generation to generation.

In 1977 my paternal grandmother, Bertha Silberberg, was at the age of eighty-eight extremely aware and loving but in failing health. She secretly dictated the following letter to her eldest son, my Uncle Ben, who was also my godfather, and asked that it be given to her family after her death. Uncle Ben read this letter to us at the ceremony honoring her memory a year after her death, and gave each family member a copy. A letter like this is often called an ethical will, and I highly recommend that you write one for your family. I have carried my copy with me almost every day since then.

The note that follows Grandma's letter is my own message to my five grandchildren, who are among my grandma's flock of great-great-grandchildren.

A Letter from My Grandma

To my beloved family: children, grandchildren, and great-grandchildren,

I am a simple Jewish woman. I believe in the eternal truths of our Torah; I believe in the Living G-d; I believe in the ultimate destiny of Israel; and I believe, with all my heart and soul, in the sanctity of the family. Your Pop and I lived our lives in accordance with these ideals and we tried, by word and deed, to teach them to you. I am proud of your response.

Since Pop left us, my life has been lonely and in recent years, filled with physical pain and suffering. In spite of this, I think of myself as blessed by Almighty G-d to have all of you near me, and to receive and accept the constant expressions of your love. No one can fully understand the joy and happiness I feel when you call, when you visit and, most of all, when you join together in family celebration.

Your Pop died with dignity, surrounded by his beloved family. I do not know whether I will be so blessed, or where or when my time will come. Whatever the circumstances, I am ready, and I will go with a full heart, secure in the knowledge that my Shema Koleinu prayer has been answered.

So—now it is time to say our last goodbyes—may G-d bless you, and keep you, and watch over you all your days, and may you be forever warmed by my eternal love.

—Grandma

A Note to My Grandchildren

Ben, Alon, Gali, David and Ely:

You are very precocious, and you soon will read this whole book, if you feel like it.

Just know how special each of you is. Even at such an early age, your intelligence, your sense of humor, your piercing eyes, and your deep souls shine bright.

Your goodness is beyond beyond.

Your Saba loves you to infinity. Maybe two infinities.

NOTES

3 Choose Success

1. Steve Jobs, commencement speech, Stanford University, June 14, 2005, accessed March 23, 2016, https://www.youtube.com/watch?v=D1R-jKKp3NA.

2. Lewis Katz, commencement speech, Temple University, Philadelphia, PA, May 15, 2014, accessed March 23, 2016, https://www.youtube.com/watch?v=ynwA-gVnpbM.

3. Ibid.

4. Malcolm S. Salter, interview by author, Cambridge, MA, April 27, 2015.

5. Glenn Segal, interview by author, Pennsauken, NJ, November 18, 2014.

6. Michael E. Gerber, *The E-Myth Revisited* (New York: HarperCollins, 1995), p. 101.

7. Peter F. Drucker, *The Effective Executive* (New York: HarperCollins, 2006), p. ix.

8. Arnold S. Daniels, *Predictive Index Management Workshop Participant Workbook and Workshop Reference Manual* (The Predictive Index, 2006).

9. See Note 2 above.

4 It's Never Too Late to Innovate

1. John C. Bogle, interview by author, Haverford, PA, February 27, 2015.

2. Scott D. Renninger, interview by author, Wynnewood, PA, December 4, 2015.

5 As Good as Your Word

1. Ed Snider, meeting with author, Philadelphia, PA, late 1990s; confirmed by email with Sanford ("Sandy") Lipstein, March 5, 2016.

2. Leslie King, email exchanges with author, December 28, 29, and 31, 2015.

3. Haim Dahan, interview by author, Tel Aviv, Israel, November 12, 2015.

6 Don't Manage—Lead!

1. Shimon Peres, meeting with author, Tel Aviv, Israel, November 17, 2015.

2. David X. Clapper, interview by author, Wynnewood, PA, November 25, 2014.

7 Ten Traits to Take You to the Top

1. David L. Cohen, interview by author, Philadelphia, PA, May 29, 2015.
2. Jeffrey A. Krames, *Lead with Humility: 12 Leadership Lessons from Pope Francis* (New York: American Management Association, 2015), p. 7.
3. Peter W. Mullin, meeting with author, 1986; confirmed by email with author, March 5, 2016.

8 Share the Risk

1. Mark I. Solomon, interview by author, Wynnewood, PA, October 22, 2015.
2. Morey H. Goldberg, interview by author, Wynnewood, PA, December 6, 2015.

9 The Golden Horseshoe

1. Bernie Marcus and Arthur Blank, *Built From Scratch* (New York: Random House, 1999), p. 37.

10 Play Fair with Your Partners

1. Michael S. Kirschner, interview by author, Wynnewood, PA, September 24, 2015.

12 Big Wallet, Big Heart, Home for Dinner

1. Alan Boal, email exchange with author, March 7, 2016.

13 Do the Right Thing

1. William A. Landman, interview by author, Wynnewood, PA, January 12, 2016.
2. Richard A. Mitchell, interview by author, Wynnewood, PA, November 24, 2015.
3. Bernie Marcus, speech to CMS Companies, Philadelphia, PA, September 13, 1995.
4. Victor H. Hammel, interview by author, Reading, PA, April 13, 2015.
5. Isadore Sharp, *Four Seasons: The Story of a Business Philosophy* (New York: Penguin, 2009), p. xi.
6. Sandra ("Sandy") L. Solmon, interview by author, Reading, PA, January 13, 2016.
7. Ibid.
8. John C. Bogle, interview by author, Haverford, PA, February 27, 2015.

14 *Acharai*: Follow Me!

1. Jerold Panas, *Mega Gifts* (Chicago: Pluribus Press, Inc., 1984), p. 198.

15 Up the Slippery Slope

1. Francesca Gino, Lisa D. Ordóñez, and David Welsh, "How Unethical Behavior Becomes Habit," *Harvard Business Review*, September 4, 2014.
2. Ibid.
3. Ibid.

4. Patricia S. Peirce, email exchange with author, February 11, 2016.

16 The Business of Family

1. Michael Shulman, interview by author, Boca Raton, FL, February 10, 2015.
2. George Cooper, *A Voluntary Tax? New Perspectives on Sophisticated Estate Tax Avoidance* (Washington, D.C.: The Brookings Institution, 1977), p. 161.

ABOUT THE AUTHOR

Paul Silberberg is president of CMS Companies, a financial services firm that *Inc.* magazine once called "The Ultimate Investment Club for Entrepreneurs." Since joining the company in 1971, two years after its inception, he helped CMS to build deep relationships with an extraordinary group of ultra-high net worth clients who, together with the firm's principals, acquired more than $12 billion in assets and $6 billion in life insurance.

As an Adjunct Professor at The Fox School of Business of Temple University, he teaches the MBA course "Leadership, Entrepreneurship, and Ethics."

He is a community leader who has received the United Way's highest honor, the Citizen Volunteer of the Year Award, as well as its CEO of the Year Award and its Tocqueville Society Award.

On behalf of disadvantaged children in Israel he became the founding U.S. chairman of Friends of Ofanim, which retrofits buses as mobile labs to educate children in remote villages, and he chaired an $80 million "Built to Last" campaign for Yemin Orde, a residential village for at-risk children.

A longtime resident of the Philadelphia area, he originated and co-chaired Philadelphia's nationally acclaimed MISSION 1000 in 1989 to arrange for Americans to visit Israel during the First Intifada (Palestinian Uprising), then created and chaired the MISSION 10,000 Task Force, a joint venture with the State of Israel, El Al Airlines, the United Jewish Communities, and the Jewish Federation of Philadelphia. He also chaired a $10 million campaign to build the Raymond and Ruth Perelman Jewish Day School in Philadelphia. Recently he joined the founding advisory board of the Satell Institute, a think tank for corporate responsibility.

Paul Silberberg earned a Bachelor of Arts degree and a Juris Doctorate from the University of Pennsylvania.

CPSIA information can be obtained
at www.ICGtesting.com
Printed in the USA
JSHW020256210323
39183JS00003BC/558

9 781683 500032